To/ Dearest Edgar.
With my love. Julia.

Christmas 2002.

IN AND OUT OF AFRICA

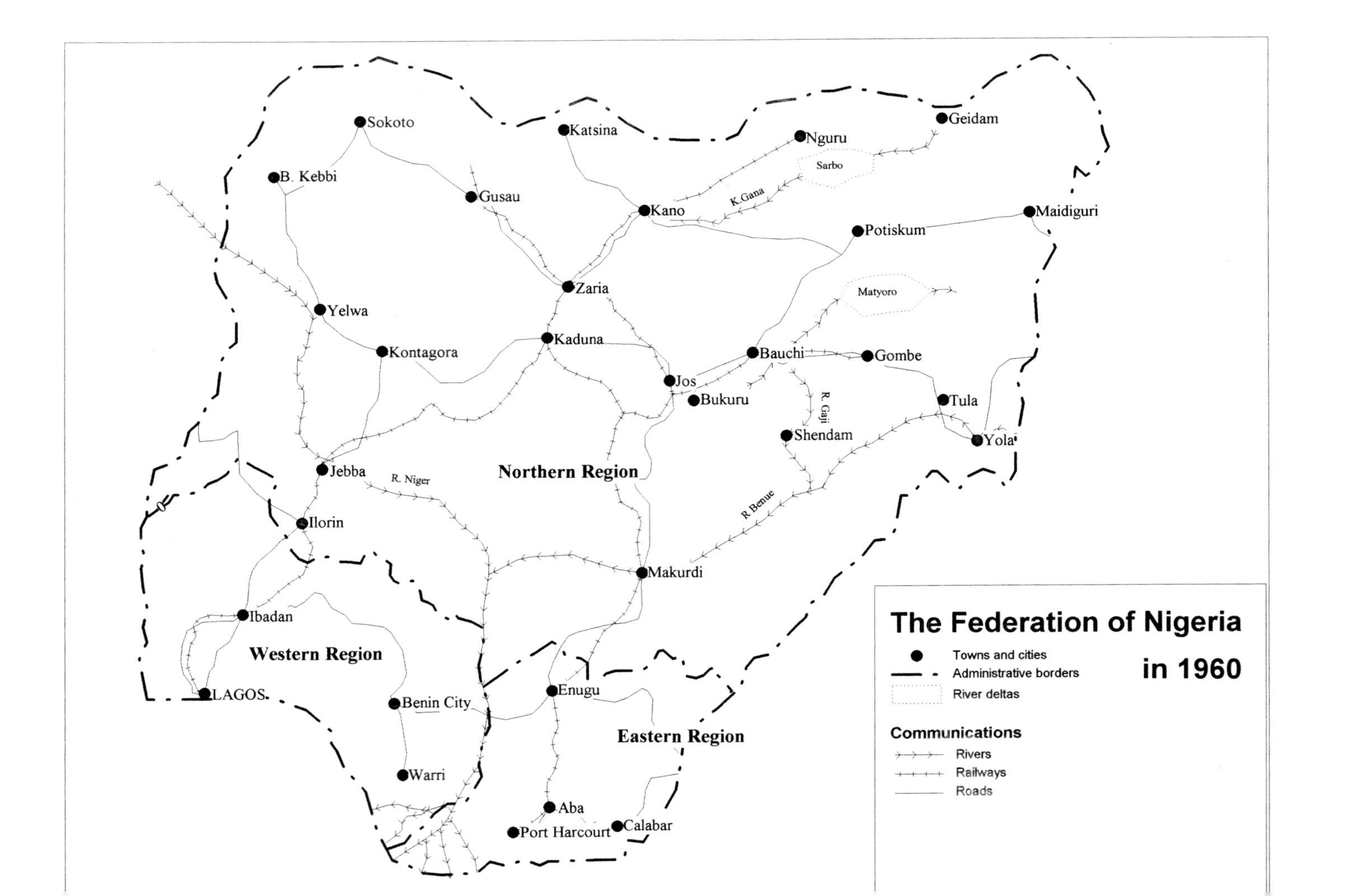
The Federation of Nigeria
in 1960
Towns and cities
Administrative borders
River deltas
Communications
Rivers
Railways
Roads
Northern Region
Western Region
Eastern Region
Sokoto
Katsina
Nguru
Geidam
B. Kebbi
Gusau
Kano
Sarbo
K. Gana
Maidiguri
Potiskum
Zaria
Matyoro
Yelwa
Kontagora
Kaduna
Bauchi
Gombe
Jos
Bukuru
Tula
R. Gaji
Shendam
Yola
Jebba
R. Niger
R Benue
Ilorin
Makurdi
Ibadan
LAGOS
Benin City
Enugu
Warri
Aba
Port Harcourt
Calabar

In and Out of Africa

Penny Aitchison

Larks Press

Published by the Larks Press
Ordnance Farmhouse
Guist Bottom, Dereham
Norfolk NR20 5PF
01328 829207
Email: Larks.Press@btinternet.com
Website: www.booksatlarkspress.co.uk

October 2002

Printed by the Lanceni Press
Garrood Drive, Fakenham

British Library Cataloguing-in-Publication Data
A catalogue for this book is available from the British Library.

ACKNOWLEDGEMENTS

I owe a great debt of gratitude to Philip Blasdale for allowing me to use his photographs of the birds of Sarbo, Northern Nigeria. My thanks go too to Dr Ross Gray and his wife, Maureen, for their account of the massacre at Vom and of Tom Leach's heroism (of which he would never have told me himself). They also contributed the wonderful lion study, we having ludicrously missed a perfect opportunity. All other photographs are my own.

ISBN 1 904006 08 6

PREFACE

Any reader of this book may well ask how I can possibly remember in such detail the events of around forty years ago. Of course I couldn't (although some will be imprinted on my mind until the day I die) without having first come across my voluminous diaries during a house move, and then discovered to my amazement that my late mother had kept more than three hundred of my letters home.

These finds gave impetus to a wish that had been floating in the back of my mind for several years. I wanted my children to know something of their parents' extraordinary experiences between 1958 and 1967 in Africa, and of their late father's dedicated and vital work in the mammoth struggle against the tsetse fly menace.

I suppose I could be said to have been one of the last batch of 'colonial wives'. I met Peter when, as a mature student from Kenya, he was at the Royal Agricultural College, Cirencester, my home town. He had been a Tsetse Control Officer in East Africa for about ten years, and served in the Kenya Police Reserve during the Mau Mau emergency.

When he decided he wanted to farm, his father suggested he take on land adjacent to his own in the White Highlands: thus I was promised 'a wonderful life in the most beautiful country in the world...' A major snag was his lack (in fact, complete absence) of capital, and he was still trying to think of some profitable course of action when the wedding was only days away.

Miraculously, it seemed at the time, a letter arrived from the Director of Veterinary Services in Northern Nigeria, offering a lucrative contract in a senior position back in the tsetse world. Peter's prayers were answered, or so he thought, and he was sure that we could save enough money to start farming after a couple of tours. A bonus was that he was needed urgently and must be ready to leave at a moment's notice.

We married, packed our bags and waited...and waited. For five months we were jobless, penniless and homeless too, had it not been for the tolerance and generosity of my far from well-off parents.

Tickets and sailing date arrived at last. In December 1958 we embarked from Liverpool on one of the old Elder Dempster 'banana boats'; we were hove-to in the Bay of Biscay for three days in the worst storm for many years, and finally reached the coast of West Africa on Christmas Eve.

And here the story, 'In and Out of Africa' begins....

Penny Aitchison 2002

AUTHOR'S NOTE

Some place-name inaccuracies are inevitable: border regions, countries too, have changed, and our own camps were naturally in remote spots, impossible to pinpoint. Any village named was just the nearest group of rural dwellings. Roads and communications have no doubt improved dramatically since that time, and travel distances may be different.

People's names are mostly as given; a very few, including two family members, have been changed.

Despite the unending series of calamities, we received kindness and help from many friends to whom I was never able to express adequate thanks: I hope my book will reach at least some of them.

I have tried to verify the accuracy of facts and captions, but I must stress that this a purely personal account. Few contemporaries remain and, sadly, no close colleagues who could correct or amplify, so I must beg the indulgence of readers who are better informed than I.

The murderous power struggle in Nigeria in the 60s was for some time the background to our own lives. My account is necessarily sketchy, drawn from our own limited experience and that of other ex-pats, as well as from contemporary journalists' reports. It is by no means intended to apportion blame to any person or group.

P.A.

CHAPTER 1

Those damn mosquito nets...I suppose they prejudiced me from the beginning. Against West Africa, Nigeria in particular. White Man's Grave...an image only too easy to conjure up when you are imprisoned. Enclosed in a greyly-glimmering semi-transparent box. When you've just been transported from briskly cold, wintry England into the enervating, damp heat of Lagos. Where was my sense of adventure? Why couldn't I get rid of the disturbing impression of being shut in a coffin? Each of the top corners of the net – the shroud – was secured by strings to the ceiling, and its ends and sides tucked tightly under the mattress of the narrow single bed.

I fidgeted listlessly. Every inch of sheet was soaked in perspiration. Sleep was impossible.

Peering through the gauze, trying to detect movement in the next bed, I could see nothing. Peter might have been five thousand miles away. Not even the outline of his body was visible. It was tempting to wake him and share my fears, but apart from being inconsiderate, I could hardly expect him, an old Africa hand, to understand my morbid fancies. It would sound silly. Childish.

There was a click and a buzz overhead, and at last the stagnant air began to move. I felt a slight, soft draught cooling my damp face. At last! This power failure had gone on for four hours, twice as long as the one earlier in the day. Still, as Peter said, I would have to get used to living without electricity, clean water and other 'conveniences'.

Just now I had to concentrate on trying to think positively and rid myself of this growing sense of isolation, of the indifference of my surroundings. Give it time. Give it time.

I began to recall specific images from the kaleidoscope of the past few days.

Freetown. We'd stepped off the boat into a Turkish bath of stifling humidity, into a land that seemed to be offering no more than token resistance to overpowering jungle, where green tentacles threatened to engulf the derelict, tin-roofed shacks lining the dusty track into the city.

We'd been told it was only a few hundred yards from the docks, an easy walk. Obviously he'd never actually done it himself. It was nearer two miles; a weary, sticky marathon in sweltering heat with an almost overwhelming sense of malign corruption.

The 'city' was a huge excrescence of squalor and decay. Filthy tumbledown huts squashed tightly together, the crannies between them packed with sprawling bodies clutching half-empty bottles. In the dark doorways patient women squatted in the dirt, suckling fly-blown infants, pounding grain in unchanging rhythm, despite the stupefying heat. Along the dusty street ragged beggars with hideous deformities stretched up imploring claws to passers-by and scraggy hens and goats scavenged in the garbage and ordure of the narrow alleys and stinking open drains. Flea-bitten donkeys, burdened with loads twice their own size, vied with ancient bicycles and rattletrap vehicles in the crowded streets.

Our throats were unbearably parched and we were relieved to be directed to the City Hotel, but that too was drab and dilapidated; walls and windows were filthy and the verandah chairs dangerously rickety. We sat for a few minutes with a bottle of Fanta Orange till the depression of our surroundings drove us outside. Unable to face the long trek back to the ship, we entrusted our fate to an ancient taxicab.

I kept my eyes closed. I'd seen enough of Freetown, and the driver, dodging donkeys, wobbly bicycles and wandering pedestrians at high speed, scared me witless as we hurtled over the bumps and ruts to the dockside.

Takoradi. An interesting comparison. Whereas Sierra Leone appears utterly indifferent to its own fate, Ghana knows perfectly well where it's going – if Takoradi is representative of the whole country. The roads were newer, wider and better constructed. Many of the little box-like houses looked fairly recently built and their tin roofs were mostly free of encroaching jungly growth. Though open drains ran in the alleys and roadsides, they were not so stagnantly unpleasant as in Freetown.

The crowds jostling in the street appeared purposeful, but less carefree. A certain tension was explained by conspicuous police presence on every street corner and in every shop doorway. There seemed to be no love lost between them and the town's inhabitants.

We soon saw why. A blue uniform suddenly appeared at the window as our taxi slowed at a junction. The driver was ordered to stop. We were not to proceed unless ...

The driver fiddled nervously with his purse and reluctantly held out a shilling. The policeman laughed derisively, knocking it out of his hand into the roadway. He spat on it. He turned and raised his voice threateningly. Sullenly, three more coins were produced and the taxi was mockingly allowed to proceed. So much for Nkrumah's 'model state'.

However, the President was evidently anxious to present a prosperous, confident façade to the outside world. We saw a showpiece craft centre, displaying exquisitely hand-carved furniture, superb artefacts, brilliantly dyed and patterned fabrics, tribal ornaments and jewellery, delicately fashioned and filigreed in beaten silver.

My spirits revived momentarily as I thought of the set of earrings and necklace Peter had bought me. But then my mind's eye saw again those ubiquitous arrogant police.

Lagos. Finally, journey's end – at least the sea-borne part. We docked at noon on Christmas Eve, but had to kick our heels in the Customs shed for four hours, before being allowed to leave.

When at last our belongings had been found, we began the first of many battles with Nigeria's officialdom. Our indignant protests were ignored as our trunks and cases were emptied unceremoniously on to the long tables. We were horrified to be charged duty on Peter's seven-year-old battered camera, on my few cosmetics, as well as on the odds and ends purchased during the voyage. Peter was made to count out his cigarettes one by one, even though it was obvious he was not exceeding his allowance.

In fact we were let off comparatively lightly. Others were hard hit. One couple had to pay pounds on an old gramophone.

Becoming inured to the sights, smells and sounds of ports on the West Coast of Africa, I was at least partly prepared for what lay ahead.

From the docks at Apapa, a taxi drove us over numerous creeks alive with dugout canoes laden with passengers being ferried to and fro, and women stepping into the water from muddy banks to wash clothes among shouting, splashing children.

The thick brown streams coiled lazily through the mangroves, whose clawing fingers seemed to be forever spreading aggressively over the feeble attempts of men to hold back their advance.

Reaching the city, I understood at once why it was a byword as 'the arsehole of Africa'. Thousands upon thousands of rusty tin-roofed shacks crowded on each other, teeming slums with steaming, stench-ridden refuse piled between them. The narrow unpaved streets swarmed with black humanity, like a huge, overturned ants' nest.

People wore every imaginable variety of clothing, perhaps assuming some outlandish European-type garment – a night-shirt, say, or a nylon petticoat – draping over it their own brilliantly-hued cloth, ragged or luxurious. The women were all very colourfully and extravagantly dressed, especially the 'mammies' presiding over their market stalls like great butterflies, decked in vividly elaborate gowns and turbans. They negotiated and bantered with the crowds with voluble good humour and commercial astuteness. Their stalls overflowed with every kind of tropical fruit, dried fish, herbs, spices, potions, charms, beads, mirrors, bangles, lengths of cloth, rugs, brightly-coloured pots and pans and much more.

Our large, smiley driver threaded the vehicle through undetectable chinks in the dense crowds, his good-natured tooting unheard in the strident cacophony of the streets. Klaxons of ancient jalopies blared their war cries as they careered amongst careless pedestrians, oblivious of junctions, traffic lights or road signs. Jaunty cyclists shouted to each other over the tumult, weaving impossible paths through the traffic, while balancing amazingly unexpected objects on their heads – suitcases, a bird cage (complete with squawking parrot), large paint pots, rolls of blankets, even a city gent's umbrella, neatly rolled.

Policemen blew unheeded whistles at milling crossroads, where piles of littered, broken vehicles bore untidy witness to the futility of their efforts.

After such a lunatic maelstrom, the European quarter of the city appeared an oasis of serenity, with its wide, clean roads, beautiful gardens and elegant houses.

The hotel did not quite match the promise of its appearance, but it would be only a matter of hours before we'd be on our way again. Tomorrow. Christmas Day, I realised with a start. Yes, Christmas 1958 would be 'celebrated' in the oddest way.

The first Christmas of our marriage was going to be spent mostly on a train, apparently.

Then we'd begin a proper life together – whatever that might mean. Already unbelievably different from anything I'd ever imagined - thousands of miles from friends, family and familiar surroundings. Now amid the alien corn ... snap out of it! Although I wouldn't feel so alone if Peter were also facing the unknown, it's a great comfort that he is used to Africa. No need to feel fearful at the start of this Great Adventure.

To Kaduna. Disappointment at having to leave the hotel after only the first course of Christmas lunch was eased by the sight of the train's facilities offered to us in consideration of Peter's status as a Government Officer.

We were surprised – and guiltily relieved – to find ourselves allocated a private compartment with easy chairs, folding bunks, toilet and washroom, while hundreds of Nigerians crammed into wooden-seated third class carriages further back.

I settled down beside the window in wondering anticipation of the excitements that must lie ahead in the 700-mile stretch northward into the hinterland.

Humanity shrank with the vegetation as the densely populated coastal belt was left behind and the villages at which the train stopped became smaller, quieter and further apart, while the trees became shorter, sparser and finally almost petered out.

Of birds or wild animals there were no signs at all and the flat emptiness of the landscape baked to biscuit-brown in the relentless heat seemed utterly lifeless, so that we looked forward to the occasional stop at tiny clusters of thatched mud huts.

Here, a crowd would materialise beside the train, and thin black arms, waving like bare branches in the wind, pushed up bowls of food to be snatched by eager hands thrust out of carriage windows.

As well as these few minutes' relief from monotony, there were endless standstills in places that seemed to have no reason to command a halt until, pulling away at last, we would catch sight of a lonely pump beside a water tank.

Red-rimmed, stinging eyes stared back at me from the little mirror in the compartment's toilet. A smut-grimed face and wild tangled hair completed the picture.

No hanging out of the window today. Night had fallen at exactly 6 p.m., as if a shutter had been dropped. Our spirits with it.

'Not quite the excitements you get from the train in Kenya,' Peter said ruefully. 'The Nairobi-Kisumu line runs through Dad's farm on Mount Eburu, where you get these terrific geysers. I remember there was an American tourist who jumped off the moving train in panic because he thought there was a huge bush fire ahead. It wasn't smoke at all, of course. Just vapour from the jets.'

'Can they be used in any way – the jets, I mean?' I fought against a rising tide of envy of the life in magical Kenya.

'Oh God, yes. There are no springs or streams on the farm, so Dad capped a few jets with galvanised pipes. As the steam travels up the pipe, it cools and condenses, so water trickles down into a trough. The old man's pretty clued up, and there's a constant supply for the house, plus enough for the cattle.'

'Like the ones we saw this afternoon?' I recalled a straggle of bony, greyish-white beasts with enormous horns wandering close to the line.

'Good Lord, no! Ours are pedigree Red Devons. Farming in the White Highlands is pretty different from here.'

Crushed by my ignorance, I lapsed into silence. Peter had many times extolled the beauty of his home country and had assured me that we'd live there as soon as he'd accumulated enough money from his Nigerian Government contract. But I knew nothing about life in East Africa. Nothing about anything beyond a very ordinary home in rural England.

The 'unknown' suddenly seemed to be looming over me, dark and infinite as the African night outside the lurching, rattling train. What was I to receive in exchange for my independence? Like a slap in the face came the realisation that, for the foreseeable future I would be led, initiate nothing, just be trailing behind. Though I'd realised that marriage to Peter would mean an end to my status as an independent, self-sufficient adult, how big would the sacrifice eventually be, on the altar of his dedication to his work and to this unfathomable land?

Morning brought little change. The faded yellow plain still stretched monotonously to the horizon, broken only by the occasional scrubby thorn tree. Sensing my disappointment, Peter tried to rally my spirits.

'Even Kenya isn't all beautiful mountains, darling. Round the coast it's pretty flat and nondescript. I had to travel a lot in that area on survey work. On the Nairobi–Mombasa line.' This struck me as funny.

'Looking for touring tsetses?' I teased.

'Believe it or not, that's quite right.' Peter was serious. 'The fly-boys and I would get on board some way beyond an infested area, then we'd keep hopping off to see if the train had picked up any little stowaways.'

'Do you mean to say you had to go round the carriages with a butterfly net or something?.' The imagination boggled.

'Not exactly. You see the little beggars attach themselves to the underside of the train to hitch a lift. They don't fly in through the windows. We'd count and record all we found, then we'd know if they were moving into new areas. Especially important if they were heading into cattle-farming country.'

'But what about wild animals?' I wanted to know. 'Don't they get sleeping sickness too?'

'No. Luckily they're immune. They're vectors – carriers – though. That was the reason – or excuse – for the terrible slaughter of game that was carried out just a few years ago.'

'In Kenya?'

'No. Fortunately ours was spared. But vast numbers were wiped out in the two Rhodesias. Not that it did much good in solving the tsetse problem.'

'How terrible.' I struggled to understand the implications. 'But at least Kenya's wildlife survived.'

'Sadly that suffered too. Other measures were used in Kenya just as devastating in the long run.'

'How? What ....'

'Hundreds of square miles of riparian vegetation – that's forest or bush alongside rivers or streams – were deliberately destroyed. Any re-growth was burnt. Just imagine the effect on game, big and small!'

The burden of my ignorance settled on my shoulders once more. However, it occurred to me that even seasoned experts were capable of appalling mistakes when faced with the complex problems of this vast land.

At last, in late afternoon, the train crawled into Kaduna. Despite it being the administrative capital of the Northern Region, its station was not much bigger than those we'd passed through en route.

We were the only Europeans to alight, and waited for several minutes on the platform surrounded by cases. Just as we began to doubt whether anyone was coming to meet us, a tall, heavily-built man in his mid-thirties came hurrying towards us. Pushing back the dark hair that flopped over his forehead, he pulled out a large handkerchief from the pocket of his khaki shorts and wiped his face, then his hand, before extending it with a somewhat embarrassed smile.

'Ah ...Peter Aitchison? And Mrs Aitchison? Welcome to Kaduna.'

He called to a waiting African to take our luggage then led us hastily to a big estate car introducing himself as he did so as Bill Kirkby, Senior Entomologist in the Animal Husbandry Ministry.

'Sorry to have to rush,' he said, rather shame-faced. 'I'll have to drop you at the Rest House and then dash home for our curry lunch.'

Peter and I exchanged glances.

'I'm awfully sorry if our arrival has put you out,' I said carefully.

'Doesn't matter a bit,' said Bill quickly. 'It's just that no one was expecting you to arrive on Boxing Day, especially as the Department closes down over Christmas, for at least two weeks.'

I could see that Peter was struggling to contain his irritation at this bit of news.

'We weren't exactly delighted to be told to leave our Lagos hotel in the middle of Christmas lunch,' he said coolly. 'However, I had written instructions to come up on this particular train. I presumed it was urgent.'

'Urgent?' Bill hooted with laughter. 'Nothing's ever urgent in this place!'

My face must have betrayed my own annoyance, as the laugh was cut short.

'Look,' he said, 'I'm sorry to appear inhospitable, but everyone has arranged social do's, so you'll just have to kick your heels in the Rest House for a bit. There'll be no one at the office for at least ten days.'

'That's OK,' said Peter. 'We'll have plenty to do, getting a vehicle organised and some touring stuff together.'

'Good show!' Bill's relief was patently obvious. 'Here we are then. See you later.'

'Some curry lunch,' I commented dryly as he drove away.

'Typical,' said the man of experience. 'In Kenya they go on till seven or eight at night. You wait. I'll soon tell you if the ones here are in the same class.'

The government Rest House, standing among shady trees, consisted of a cluster of chalets and provided a modicum of comfort. Simply furnished sleeping quarters with a tiny bathroom.

I couldn't wait. 'There's a bath!' I shouted gleefully. 'Me first!'

I turned on the tap as far as it would go, only to see a few brown drops fall from it, then stop.

'Oh no!' I wailed.

Peter put his head round the door.

'What's up? Oh damn ... look!' he pointed.

There was a hand-scrawled scrap of paper stuck below the mirror: 'SORRY FOR NO WATER'.

'I'll just have to ask the steward at Reception for some and ask about meals at the same time. I think I noticed a dining room ... Oh God! Look at us!'

I stood beside him in front of the mirror and scarcely recognised the scarecrow couple I saw: hair sticking out, stiff and dull, faces dirty-grey, streaked higgledy-piggledy with smuts from the smoking train, the skin round the eyes white in contrast, giving them a strange, startled look.

Our shocked silence lasted several seconds before we burst out laughing.

'No wonder we didn't get invited back to Bill what's-his-name's for curry lunch,' Peter said.

CHAPTER 2

Ten days of boredom and frustration were an unpromising start to our 'new life'.

Without transport, friends or contacts – other Ministry officers apparently unaware of our arrival – we sweated it out, quite literally, until the commercial area of the town reluctantly revived, and we could begin, we hoped, to make preparation for 'bush life'.

We quickly learned by bitter experience that to maintain sanity in this country required the greatest patience and unflappability.

First, we were surprised to discover that this important town boasted only two shops, both disappointing.

In the main store, Kingsway, stocks were extremely limited as well as expensive and the service maddeningly poor. The girls at the counters lounged, chewing, and could scarcely be bothered to reply to a customer's query. Nine times out of ten they'd say an item was 'out of stock', even if it was in full view on a shelf behind them.

Peter, whose years in East Africa had taught him exactly what his 'touring' needs would be, abandoned the hassle and decided to wait until he could get advice on sources from colleagues.

We switched our efforts to the transport problem. Government loans were available to 'essential users', which here meant everybody, so Peter quickly negotiated with the one garage, U.T.C., for a tough estate car of the make that had served him well over some of Kenya's toughest terrain.

As soon as the H.Q. of the Ministry of Animal Husbandry & Veterinary Services stuttered reluctantly back into life, Peter enquired about safari gear and was advised to try Jos, recommended as an interesting and much better commercial centre where he'd be more likely to find what he needed. Or he could ask in Bauchi, where we were to be stationed, if anyone was selling off gear before leaving the country, as by far the best equipment was second-hand and there was always plenty about, due to the rapid turnover of 'ex-pats'.

The advice was confirmed when we heard, at last, from Geoff Wilson, Director of Veterinary Services. It was he who had recruited Peter from Kenya, where they'd worked together. He and his wife Maureen (also a doctor, but of medicine) were full of apologies for the miserable reception we'd received. They themselves had only just returned from spending Christmas with friends in Jos.

'You'll love the place,' smiled Maureen. 'There are hills, scenery, a beautiful hotel – everything Kaduna lacks, in fact.'

'But your house is lovely,' I said, my optimism having been restored by a sophisticated drinks party in an elegant, spacious drawing room, with french windows overlooking a large shady garden, aglow with bougainvillea, allamanda and canna lilies, despite the fact that this was the height of the dry season.

'Yes, we're lucky to have this, but I'm afraid I don't much enjoy the social life here in Kaduna – an endless round of coffee mornings, bridge sessions and cocktail parties. It gets pretty boring after a while, so I'm very glad to have my own practice.'

There was no time for us to discover whether we shared her views. Suddenly instructions arrived for us to travel to Bauchi, via Jos, immediately, so the following day we left early for the 170-mile drive to Jos.

Despite being a main road, it was un-tarred; the usual orangey laterite. By 9a.m., it was baking hot, and I realised I hadn't seen a single cloud in the sky since setting foot in Africa. The landscape that had accompanied our train journey like a tedious companion who exasperatingly refuses to leave and give you some respite, had merely waited in the shadows and was again a deadening presence, dogging us.

The few passing vehicles sent up clouds of dust that blinded and choked us, maddening to endure because of the enforced gentle 'running-in' of our new car. Particularly alarming were the 'mammy-wagons', ragged canvas-topped trucks packed to the eyeballs with shouting, gesticulating Africans, many of whom clung to the outside of the lorry, the back, the top and sides, which were usually decorated with earnest exhortations: – 'Bless me O God!' – 'No telephone to Heaven!' - 'Oh Nigeria! Why worry!'.

This last typified the sublime confidence of the drivers whose rickety vehicles swayed terrifyingly, careering at speed from one side of the road to the other. One slowed, bumpily, shortly after overtaking us and we saw to our amazement a boy of about eleven leap from the cab with a large chunk of wood. He ran ahead of the truck, then waited for it to come alongside, when he dextrously shoved it in front of the nearside front wheel. The lorry lurched to a stop, almost toppling as all the passengers leapt out and squatted by the roadside.

Fortunately I realised the significance of the posture, having inadvertently caught sight of it several times around Kaduna, and quickly averted my eyes.

At last a dim shape loomed in the hazy distance – Jos Plateau. Now we'd see whether it lived up to the eulogies we'd heard.

After the earliest military expeditions which reached the edge of the Plateau, 4,300 feet above sea level, at the start of the 20th century, mineral prospectors arrived, who penetrated further and discovered deposits of alluvial tin. They also found a much healthier climate than in the plains below. Originally, tin had been smelted and worked by men of the Hausa tribe. From furnaces, the molten metal ran into moulds made from damp ashes pressed round a number of straws set parallel to each other. The rods of tin so formed were sold by local traders at Ibi.

With the introduction of modern mining methods, production grew over the next forty years from a few dozen pounds per annum, to more than 17,500 tons.

Other minerals, columbite, tantalite and galena were also mined.

In the midst of this new prosperity, Jos developed as the mining community's main trading centre, with its own airport, hospital, hotels and cinemas.

Prior to the expansion of the mining industry, the Plateau had been inhabited mostly by pagan tribes who were constantly subject to raids by Arab or Muslim slavers. Captives were taken, either across the Sahara desert, or to the northern towns of Nigeria.

We hoped to be able to visit one of the villages of the Birom tribe, who live in small grass-thatched huts fenced with cactus-like plants. Families each cultivate small plots of yams, guinea corn, bullrush millet and 'Acha', a grass-like crop which they brew into a potent beer.

We had to agree that Jos was a big improvement on Kaduna, and though also created by European enterprise, was without the artificiality one sensed in the latter.

Kaduna (the name is the plural of 'Kada' – crocodile) was established as his headquarters by Lugard in 1911, in an area entirely devastated by the slave trade. The site had the great advantage of permanent water, being on the Kaduna River, and the town was planned on model lines: houses were built in a formal grid pattern, and impressive administrative buildings erected, the principal one being Lugard Hall, the seat of the Northern Region government.

Here in Jos, the thriving expatriate mining community made itself comfortable with imposing homes and lovely gardens, an exclusive luxurious Country Club and a variety of excellent sporting facilities, though here, as in the rest of Nigeria, no European was allowed to own land, so there were – and are – no permanent 'settlers'.

However, when we arrived sticky, filthy and stained the colour of freshly-pulled carrots from the laterite dust of our journey, despite the car windows having been closed, we were far from impressed to find pinned to the bathroom door of our Rest House accommodation, the by-now familiar notice: 'Owing to water shortage ...'

We cleaned up with the help of a bucket brought by a steward, then ventured optimistically into the centre to find these 'much better shops'.

Perhaps because the town was unfamiliar to us, we tramped with increasing frustration round dismal, crowded stores, just like those in Kaduna and with similarly churlish, indifferent staff.

We were almost too tired to eat supper and crawled early under our mosquito nets, only to discover that our room was directly over the bar, and the racket from boozy ex-pats kept us awake until long after midnight.

Next morning, the car still being serviced at U.T.C., we tried to complete our shopping.

A good place for groceries was an Indian-owned store, Chellaram's, where we ordered an enormous quantity of supplies and now feeling more confident, we ventured into the local market. Immediately we were surrounded – presumably because we were recognised as newcomers – by persistent vendors who blocked our path, pushing their wares into our faces, bangles, beads, brassware, wood carvings, horn ornaments, goat and camel skin bags, as well as a variety of fruit and vegetables surprising in this dry climate and dessicated countryside.

Back at the Rest House, Peter began to be alarmingly sick and we spent a wretched night. My mind was full of morbid fears that he would die and leave me stranded and desolate in this ghastly country.

In the morning, with Peter scarcely strong enough to totter to the car, I drove him to the hospital where a boyish Dr Brooks cheerfully diagnosed probable jaundice, adding that we must not attempt to continue to Bauchi if the diagnosis was confirmed.

Shattered, I drove Peter back to the Rest House, tucked him into bed and returned to the Clinic for the long wait for the test results. My hands were coldly clammy despite the heat and I jumped up every time a white coat appeared.

After two hours Dr Brooks emerged, smiling and reassuring. It had been a false alarm. 'Two pills every four hours for three days and he'll be fine.'

I was reluctant to trust him. He seemed far too young.

HELLO! HELLO!! HELLO!!!

THE NIGERIAN MORDERN BARBARS SALOON

DOWN STREET CF OLYMPIC, BUKURU.

You are welcomed to the above mentioned workshop, for a Neat, Decent and acttractive Hair cut both Africans and Europeans respectively. And at the same time we are proud of our complete instruments such as Electric Chairs, Cumbs, Clippers and Shaving Razor in addition Air Condi-tion.

COME ONE COME ALL.

Advertising Nigerian style

CHAPTER 3

Bauchi. Two days later, Peter was sufficiently improved for us to tackle the last leg of our journey.

We were assured there was marvellous scenery en route. 'Watch out for the infamous Mile 30: there's a precipitous drop on either side of a devilishly winding road,' enthused a white-haired, leathery-skinned old-timer at the Rest House, but Peter's years of surveying and exploring the wilder regions of East Africa made him even more sceptical than me. It came as no surprise that the odd steep, sharp bend we encountered scarcely matched those of the West Country lanes at home and I was hard put to it to equate the barren, rocky heights with 'marvellous scenery'.

Soon back on the familiar plain, by late afternoon we'd reached our destination – Bauchi.

All we could see was a Rest House, under a cluster of neem trees, a Club building and a small block of flats, incongruously enough, opposite. No other buildings were in sight.

'At least there's a tennis court,' I said.

'And the flats look pretty new,' said Peter, 'though it's funny to find flats in a bush station.'

We followed the steward into a little chalet in the Rest House and I rushed to the bathroom.

'Guess what?' I called.

'Don't tell me. Not again.'

The steward brought a bucket.

We inspected the flats next morning. There were only four, two up and two down, the upper ones with balconies and those on the ground floor had a small paved area in the front. The building was a small oblong block of grey stone flanked by a few skimpy trees. There had been an attempt in the past to create a garden in a tiny square in the middle of the paving, but all that remained were withered sticks. Presumably no one stayed long enough to bother.

At present, only one of the flats was occupied and Mrs Peters was obviously delighted to have neighbours. An anxious, prematurely-aged woman in her mid-thirties, her husband on contract to the Public Works Department, she was unhappy at being dragged out to West Africa, and longed to be safely back amongst friends and family, shops and cinemas in Islington.

As we tackled the chore of cleaning the filthy rooms in the upper flat allocated to us, she revived us with frequent cups of tea, and even insisted on scrubbing the kitchen floor herself. Fortunately the 'harmattan', the dust-laden wind from the Sahara, was blowing quite strongly, and brought some relief from the heat. Without fans or air-conditioning, since there was no electricity, the flats were suffocatingly hot for much of the year.

Mrs Peters waxed lyrical over the hot water system which, like the cooker, was fuelled by kerosene.

'Our Ken'll show you. It's ever so easy.'

Privately we doubted it and sure enough, having carefully primed and lit the wick following the instructions to the letter, the pressure gauge refused to budge. Grubby and weary after the day's exertions, we gave up.

'Sorry darling. It's back to the Rest House tonight with a bucket again. This thing's obviously faulty and I'll have to get the P.W.D. to send someone to fix it.'

'Oh well,' I shrugged. 'It's not as if we've moved in properly. Let's hope they do it tomorrow.'

Early next morning we found a Public Works Department lorry outside the flat, and two Hausas were unloading furniture. Not much; the Government provides only the barest essentials – dining table and chairs, a couple of wooden-armed easy chairs and beds. Everything is so standardised you could forget where you're stationed – moves are frequent but furnishings and surroundings remain substantially the same.

Unpacking our trunks, I heard a quiet knock and found at the door an elderly African, small, grey and wiry, with enormous rolling eyes and a toothless smile. He was standing smartly at attention, in a well-pressed green uniform of wide tunic over loose trousers ending just above the ankle. Barefoot.

'Scoos, pleese, madam; you wish for velly good cook, yes?'

'Well, perhaps ... Can you come back later?'

'Yes pleese, madam.' The wide grin remained. So did he. I asked his name.

'Me Wasinda. Velly good cook. Meestah Corta, sah, he sen' me you. He cook ma brudder.'

'Cooked your brother!' I was obviously not understanding properly.

'Yessah. Ma brudder much too good cook too.'

'Oh, I see. Well, come back this afternoon, then.'

'Yes pleese. Me ready to start now.'

'Good. Thank you Wasinda.'

Going to the door with him, I noticed two other men hanging round the flat entrance. Had they come to fix the water heater? 'Excuse me,' I called. They glanced in my direction and wandered off towards the Rest House.

An hour later, hearing voices in the compound below, I looked down from the bedroom window to see the same two men sitting gossiping, leaning against the wall surrounding the patio. Uneasily, but trying to be hopeful, I called down to them, but there was again no response, so rather crossly, I got on with the unpacking.

Nearly an hour later there was a knock at the door. One of the same two men stood there.

'I come mend heater for bath,' he said. He took the cylinder away and returned with it after a full hour. Watching him replace it, I looked vainly for some signs of repair. There were none and, as I expected, when he lit the wick, nothing happened. He shrugged, unhitched it and disappeared.

Over the next two days, this pantomime was repeated three more times.

'And all that was needed was a bit of solder,' grumbled Peter, when at last I turned the tap on with a flourish. 'If I'd had the stuff, I'd have done it myself in two minutes.'

Wasinda was taken on and was cheerfully confident about the little kerosene stove in the kitchen and when we'd installed the bottled gas fridge bought in Jos, and filled up the big filter with boiled water, I began to breathe more easily.

Our first 'social engagement' was an invitation to dinner with the Resident, a charming, public-school man with an elegant Austrian wife who more than hinted at family connections with European aristocracy. Both seemed rather out-of-place in a bush station.

The other guests, who came from a wide area, were all Government officers, or on secondment from the UK, and were working in forestry, education, agriculture or medicine. Without exception they expressed utter frustration at the mind-boggling inefficiency of the country, the never-ending battle against dirt, heat, disease and above all, boredom. New arrivals were greeted enthusiastically as a welcome diversion. We, on the other hand, were amused by the scandalous gossip bandied about – inevitable in a small community where there was nothing else to talk about.

I contemplated the company, wondering who it might be interesting to know. One of the two bachelors there, William, a thin, dark Forestry man of barely 35, was 'three sheets to the wind' after his first whisky and sat with his eyes fixed upwards, lids half-closed and flickering, and spoke not a word all evening. His only movement being to reach for his glass with a shaking hand.

'He's given up solid food entirely,' said a quiet voice and I found myself in conversation with Charlie Hall, a 'grass widower' who was a Yard Superintendent in the P.W.D., out here on his own because his wife couldn't stand West Africa and remained securely in Edinburgh, while her husband battled with more problems than most in his position. At first it was amusing to listen to so many stories – usually barbed – about ex-pats in his 10-year experience, but he moved his chair embarrassingly close, and began whispering sharp confidences about the present company and proffering advice as to who I should or should not get to know better. It was a relief to take the chance, when it came, of slipping away, and I joined Peter with new friends, David and Charlotte, who were, like us, keen tennis players.

Charlotte was to prove a most useful friend, helping me with curtain-making – an urgent task which I hadn't anticipated – and advising us how to get a monthly supply of chilled foods ('cold-store') from Jos, which could be ordered from the local Chellaram's.

It would be a relief to have a change from the ever-lasting diet of tinned stuff, which we'd been living on. Admittedly the local fruit was a joy – mangoes, bananas, pawpaws and citrus, though the vegetables seemed limited to stringy runner beans and dry carrots. I had quickly become accustomed to the previously hated taste of onions, added in quantity to everything in order to disguise doubtful flavours.

'Local meat isn't too bad,' said Charlotte, 'so long as you've got a cook who knows what he's doing. Don't go to the market yourself, unless you've got a very strong stomach: the animals are slaughtered in full view, then skinned and cut up on the slab. Absolutely revolting. Covered in flies. Blood everywhere, and more vultures round the slab than slaughtermen.'

Next morning I resolved to test Wasinda's astuteness at the market, and sent him to buy a leg of mutton. At six that evening, as we dawdled over our 'sun-downers', a faint but unsavoury odour began seeping in through the door to the kitchen. The door opened and immediately the room was filled with a horrible pungency as the grinning Wasinda bore in a blackened joint with a suspiciously long, bony leg sticking up from the dish.

Sitting at the table, my stomach turned over. Peter grimaced.

'Wasinda!' he shouted.

'Yessah.' The cook's grin was wider than ever.

'Where the hell did you get this? Don't you know the difference between mutton and goat!'

'This bes' mutton, sah! Ver' ver' bes' mutton, sah! Me buy only bes' mutton for madam, sah!'

'Just don't ever buy goat again, Wasinda,' Peter said, subsiding into muted exasperation realising he wasn't going to win any arguments against that confident grin, and closing the subject firmly.

'I'm beginning to have my doubts about that chap,' he said, as Wasinda, still smiling, retreated to the kitchen. 'It's a pity we can't check out his reference as his last family have gone back to the UK. Also, I don't see what training is going on, where Dalmia is concerned.'

Dalmia was the 'small boy', an essential part of every household, and had come attached to Wasinda. 'Small boys' always did the bulk of the chores, including the menial ones, which were below the dignity of a cook. Ours, a six-foot sixteen-year-old, was very raw indeed, and his English was limited to 'Yes, madam, I understan' too good', which invariably meant he hadn't understood a word. He had come with a 'certificate' which Wasinda assured us was proof he was a 'ver'good boy', but we soon doubted whether he had ever worked for a European family before, especially when on his first morning, I discovered him cleaning the bath vigorously with my facecloth, liberally sprinkled with Jeyes Fluid.

Wasinda needed constant reminders to impress on Dalmia that he must wash his hands before laying the table, or helping with food preparation (the absence of water supply to most African homes meant washing hands was not something done very often).

I disliked having to keep all our stores locked up, but discovered early on, that our two chaps regarded their employers' goods as fair game, even though by local standards they were well paid, and had, in addition, basic food-stuffs which I doled out daily.

Besides his neglect of his 'training' responsibilities, Wasinda was also causing anxiety by his frequent and prolonged absences from the house. His own quarters were in a nearby compound and whenever he was needed, Dalmia had to be sent to find him, which usually took a very long time.

After some weeks of poorly cooked, often belated meals, I suggested to Peter that I should do the cooking myself.

'Oh no, that's *not* on, darling,' he said firmly.

'I think I could manage that funny oil stove,' I insisted.

'Perhaps, but when we leave Bauchi, probably quite soon, the next place will probably have a 'black monster' in the kitchen – the usual smoky, temperamental wood stove. Fiendishly hot in this climate too.'

While I mentally listed the range of complaints I had against Wasinda, he went on, 'For another thing, I'm going to be spending an enormous amount of time away on safari, doing tsetse surveys, and I have to take a cook with me.'

I didn't look at him. This kind of life was not at all what I'd thought I had pledged myself to at our marriage service in a quiet English village some months previously. I wasn't sure if I could cope.

'Well, I hope Wasinda won't let you down,' I said. He was not after all put to the test, as the next day's events decided the issue.

We had invited guests to dinner – the Resident and his wife, David and Charlotte, also Charlie Hall, who had shown us almost too much hospitality since our arrival in Bauchi.

I prepared a simple grapefruit starter and a mousse dessert early in the day, and asked Wasinda to roast a chicken for the main course. Half an hour before the guests were due to arrive, I put my head round the kitchen door, shrieked and slammed it shut again.

'Peter!' I screamed.

'What the devil's the matter?' He dashed half-dressed out of the bedroom.

'Well may you ask,' I said weakly. 'Devil is the operative word ...' I waved faintly at the kitchen.

'What on earth do you mean?' He strode to the door.

'Look out!' I shouted. Too late.

A dirty, grey projectile hurtled past him, feathers flying and squawking, its long, scraggy legs going like the clappers as it hurled itself from one side of the room to the other, pursued by a lumbering, inebriated Wasinda, waving a bottle in one hand and a cleaver in the other.

'Get *out!*' shouted Peter. '*Get out this minute!*'

He seized both bottle and cleaver and frog-marched the hapless cook none too gently to the back door, propelling him down the steps to ground level, where he released his grasp. He looked disgustedly down at the inert figure crumpled at his feet mouthing 'Shagi! Shagi!' an inane smile on his face.

'Dalmia!' shouted Peter. 'Where the hell are you?'

'Comin', sah.' The lanky figure stumbled out of the servants' quarters, pulling on his tunic. As his head emerged through the opening, his eyes became great white saucers and his mouth dropped open as he recognised the figure on the ground.

'Dalmia, catch that bird!' Peter ordered. The blank, hypnotised eyes came to life and followed the direction of Peter's pointing finger.

'Me catch'em plenty quick, sah!' he replied, catching the urgency of the situation and hared off in hot pursuit ...

Somehow, disaster was averted.

There was a large tin of ham in the cupboard and I offered up a silent prayer of thanks that starter and dessert were safely in the fridge.

When Dalmia returned, I quickly showed him how to cook rice and then concocted a sauce using a tin of soup and the few limp vegetables I found in a sack behind the kitchen door.

Peter had just finished clearing up the last desperate droppings from the terror-stricken bird, when the first car scrunched up the gravel drive.

Our Vanguard on a bridge that had been submerged two hours previously

CHAPTER 4

Within a very short time of arriving in Bauchi, Peter's initial tsetse survey gave me my first taste of real 'bush' life, although this one was less primitive than expected. We drove over 150 miles of narrow, rough, corrugated road through what seemed to my inexpert eyes, unchanging, low, mostly evergreen woodland, the 'doka' trees small by English standards, and too widely-spaced for their canopies to interlace.

At our destination, Mallam Sidi, I was surprised to find a new-ish Rest House, a simple thatched rondavel. Peter had made sure my initiation into his world of 'touring' would not be too uncomfortable. Maman, the new steward who had joined us after Wasinda's disgrace, quickly made it habitable with camp beds and folding chairs, then disappeared to find water and to build a temporary stove in the little 'kitchen' hut nearby. A second hut provided sanitation, which I discovered on venturing out – braving the curiosity of the dozens of locals who materialised out of nowhere to watch our every move – consisted of a bucket and a hole in the ground.

Back in the rondavel, I was alarmed at the sight of countless lizards running round the walls or tight-roping along the narrow roof beams, but Peter assured me they were harmless and I was quickly fascinated by their beady eyes and purple skin, providing bright flashes on the whitewashed walls and grey floor. They disappeared as darkness fell, and we sat in the bare, circular room, with the oil lamp casting deep shadows around us and the rhythm of distant drums in our ears.

When Maman had filled the low canvas bath, I stripped and lowered myself into the cold water uneasily. A succession of tiny 'plops' beside me were a puzzle till I looked up at the roof timbers and saw a long line of earwigs steadily crawling to the centre post, then nose-diving into the bath! Having landed in the water, they swam to the side, crawled up the canvas and trotted sedately along the narrow rim for a few inches and at a pre-determined spot, crawled carefully down to floor level, then hastened to join the long queue for the exit.

It was as if they were on an annual migration and were taking advantage of a short cut via the bath, instead of the long way round the walls to reach the door.

It was comforting, oddly enough, to have these familiar creatures sharing my bath ...

That night, the first of many 'on tour', I lay long awake, uncomfortably tossing in the narrow camp bed, imprisoned by the grey mesh of the mosquito net, tightly tucked in) and oppressed by the ceaseless wailing and drumming from the nearby village.

Peter, as usual, fell asleep almost instantly.

Each morning, Peter left at barely dawn, leaving me to struggle to fill purposeless hours, without books or music to cushion the emptiness of my existence until his return early in the afternoon. Then we shared a meal – inevitably out of tins – and retired to our camp beds for a siesta. The steward produced a pot of tea at around 4.30 p.m., after which Peter concentrated on his work diary and reports which he typed with one finger until 'sun-downers' at 6.30 p.m.

It occurred to me that if I could learn to type, I could be useful, and my life would not seem so utterly meaningless. It was difficult to think of 'news' to fill the half-dozen or so letters I wrote every morning, once early impressions had been described.

I stretched a tea towel over the keys, propped up a faded Pitman key-card found tucked under the battered cover and sitting at the camp table under the shady tamarind beside the Rest House, I concentrated fiercely on making my fingers match the pattern.

A few hours spent staring at this static activity eventually bored the crowd of child spectators who gathered outside every morning, and they trickled back to their village – to my relief. Their wide-eyed curiosity, never satisfied, weighed on my conscience, but I was an alien from another world, probably they'd never seen a white woman before, and very seldom a man. We had no means of communication. Neither Peter nor I could speak Hausa, but while he could attempt the basics with his 'mallams', the more educated of his workforce, I had no one to advise, teach or encourage me.

At least, these were the excuses I made to myself over the following months, but the truth was that the monotonous isolation of my situation stifled any initiative. Even my feeble efforts at touch-typing were only produced by a sense of desperation rather than 'pro-active thinking'.

I was reminded of Evelyn Waugh's reflection on his own boredom in the tropics: '...days as black as damnation; a handful of fine ashes thrown into the eyes; a blanket over the face; a mass of soft clay knee-deep...'. And that referred to just four days!

Before returning to Bauchi, Peter had to visit Gombe, so when everything had been packed up, we headed out, and by midday reached the Residence, where he had to make a duty call.

After half an hour, during which time I was left waiting in what shade I could find outside, Peter returned, fuming. The man had been pompous and overbearing, he said, and even presumed to tell him his job! Worse, he insisted that Peter move to Gombe, though on what authority he couldn't imagine.

The trouble was undoubtedly caused by the circumstances surrounding Peter's arrival on the tsetse scene. Dr Wilson, it transpired, had neglected to inform anyone of the appointment, hence no one was prepared to pay Peter's salary, work with him, or advise him professionally on local conditions. It was to be many months before these difficulties were sorted out; meanwhile, he had no ammunition to fire back at little Hitlers like Hubert Hawkes-Fry.

He was anxious to find out from HQ whether there was any official basis for this directive, but communication with Kaduna was slow and unreliable. However, Bill Kirkby appeared at the flat the morning after our return and confirmed our fears. Yes, Gombe would shortly be our next base. From the little we'd seen of it, and the reports we'd heard, it would not be a pleasant experience.

I was delighted that Bill had brought his wife, Audrey. It was such a change to be in company, especially female, though I was hard put to it to make our meagre store of food stretch to lunch. There'd been no chance to stock up since our return yesterday.

I thought we'd done well with a reasonable first course, till Peter said suddenly, 'I don't know about you, but I'm still *ravenous*!' At that moment Maman came in with dessert, not the big, filling pudding I'd asked him to make, but a tiny dish of mousse – barely enough for a teaspoon each!

Survey work now began in earnest, not easy in an area devoid of paths, even animal tracks, where Peter and his team hacked through unmapped flat bush country which lacked ridges, valleys or any features to help him plot his courses. He was away for days on end.

Meanwhile, I found myself unexpectedly useful to the half-dozen or so ex-pat wives on the station, none of whom had seen a hairdresser for months, some even over a year. On the strength of brief and limited experience in a salon during a College vacation, I dared to wield scissors and rollers; even did home perms.

In the flat, on my own, coping with the servants was a trial, though I soon stopped feeling guilty about employing them since I could not have done the housework and cooking on my own.

Dalmia's inexperience led to such exasperating 'accidents' as, for example, having burning coals from the charcoal iron dropped on to our precious, new bed-linen. Maman bravely tried to mend the holes, but they were impossible to repair.

I spent many hours sewing curtains by hand, during daylight hours, then often played tennis in the hour before darkness fell, when the heat was less intense.

Before the move to Gombe, Peter took me out on a five-day tour to Alkalere, where he knew there was a Rest House – of sorts. It was a step-up from a mud hut with its corrugated iron roof, partly covered with dishevelled thatch, a series of tiny rooms linked by door-less doorways. There were separate huts for Maman's quarters and for the 'kitchen', where he made a fire between stones.

Going to the loo was rather an adventure. It was just a wooden box over a hole in the ground, which held a bucket; a lizard had taken up residence on the 'seat', and refused to budge until shooed off! A very active hornet's nest hung a few inches above one's head and there was a suspicious-looking hole beside one's feet which I watched constantly, expecting a snake to appear. I didn't take a book in, and Peter didn't fancy doing his half-hour Hausa study in there, either!

We returned to Bauchi to await instruction for the projected move to Gombe and to join the general indignation of ex-pats at the news that taxes were to rise sharply: prices for essentials, including petrol and food, had already increased by almost a third. We met no one who wasn't extremely pessimistic about Nigeria's future for new arrivals like ourselves.

The main worry was that self-government was imminent and independence soon to follow, a prospect surprisingly unwelcome to quite a large number of indigenous northerners, who felt unprepared. Already, apparently, there were signs of tension among the three Regions, East, West and North, and traditional inter-tribal suspicion was heightened by rumours of corruption in high places. The feudal Emirs of the predominantly Muslim North, by far the largest region geographically, were not prepared for their authority, strengthened by the British administration over the previous sixty years, to be undermined by a National Government.

Our concern about national issues was overshadowed by more personal worries: non-payment of Peter's salary and expenses as well as the evident lack of planning and leadership at the top of his Department. His confidence was shaken by the news that several key research scientists were quitting because they felt they were getting a raw deal.

My own problems were daily irritations, not helped by an inability to make our steward understand that serving gritty onion stew twice a day, every day of the week, was just not acceptable.

I had to face the prospect of a long spell on my own as Peter prepared for his first major safari, taking fifteen porters, two guides, as well as the survey team, to the Gaji River swamp area.

During the first day's trek, they passed through a long-abandoned village, which, one of the guides told him, had once been thriving, but had been cursed by a neighbouring headman, who accused the villagers of stealing his best bull. Many unexplained deaths followed, and the terrified inhabitants quickly left their homes and built a new settlement many miles away.

Peter wondered privately if the deaths might in fact have been caused by an epidemic of sleeping sickness, as the old village was in a tsetse-infested zone.

A first camp was established in the fringing forest of the Gaji River, relatively cool, with water, although filthy, near at hand. Each morning, camp was struck, the porters directed to a pre-arranged rendezvous while the survey patrols began systematically collecting information concerning tsetse distribution – density, species and habitat. *Glossina morsitans* was fairly easy to catch in the butterfly nets used by the 'flyboys', but *tachinoides*, much more active, was very elusive.

Four or five hours of exhausting, thirsty work ended when the team caught up with the porters, and the search for a fresh campsite began. As soon as it was established, Peter, after a short siesta, set about recording and collating the data, and organising the next stage of the survey.

Peter with foot porters on safari

After a week, the long return trek began. Striking camp by 6.30 a.m., they walked through the bush for sixteen miles before stopping in the midday heat – a considerable achievement for the heavily loaded porters – another camp set up and dismantled again next morning for a similar stretch. At noon they finally reached the village where the vehicles had been left and the safari ended with a two hour bumpy ride for the fifty-four miles back to Bauchi.

While Peter was away, I'd been struggling against severe 'tummy palaver', so reluctant to clear that he insisted I should see the station doctor.

The surgery was at the local hospital where we found a line of prefabricated buildings and a long queue at 'Out-Patients' sitting cheerfully in the shade outside.

Inside the compound, alongside the wards, were sitting the relatives of the 'In-Patients' – whole families who remained throughout the patient's stay, supplying food and comfort.

Some people came with the most trivial complaints, others had terrible diseases for which they refused treatment. It was not uncommon for a sick person to decide to leave his bed and the hospital long before he had recovered and it was difficult for a doctor to persuade a patient to follow instructions or take the medicine given. The lack of clean water and sanitation in their homes was the greatest block to successful treatment, since basic rules of hygiene could hardly apply without them.

CHAPTER 5

Sarbo, Hidden Paradise. News arrived that a house would be ready for us in Gombe in the third week of March, but before then, Peter was required to visit a colleague in a remote area north of Potiskum. To my relief his camp could accommodate me as well, so I looked forward to a change from lonely days in the flat.

We left early, hoping to get the worst of the journey over before the fiercest heat of the day, but we had to endure 200 miles of corrugations and ruts through the endless, featureless plain with which we had become all too familiar. The only sight of interest was that of half-a-dozen camels being loaded in a village en route, much against their inclinations. One in particular was being held down by three men, yet still tried to bite everyone within reach, his neck twisting and bending like a great snake. He reminded me of Alice in Wonderland and the pigeon.

Reaching Potiskum in the early afternoon, we searched for the road to Yerwa, another thirty miles on. To our dismay it turned out to be a treacherous sandy track across a desolate wilderness, where great drifts of sand which threatened to overwhelm us made progress painfully slow. We began to fear that we would be trapped by darkness.

Just as we reached anxious despair, we suddenly found ourselves in a shady forest glade, and were amazed to see a mother warthog and her two sweet, ugly babies scamper away from us in panic.

Our guide, whom we'd collected in Potiskum, directed us through a maze of paths until we reached a clearing where, by a solidly constructed Robinson Crusoe hut of grass thatch supported on rough poles, we met our host, a smiling, gangly entomologist of thirty-odd, who welcomed us warmly.

Philip's camp was right on the bank of an old watercourse, now a long, winding lake. Sitting in the open end of the 'lounge', we looked directly down on to the water, delightedly viewing the comings and goings of an incredible variety of birds. A sudden racket in a nearby thicket announced the arrival of a playful group of monkeys, and the solid splash from the same quarter was a sign, Philip said, that the six-foot monitor lizard, whose home was in the bank, did not want disturbance and had taken to the water.

Philip was a keen and knowledgeable ornithologist for whom three years in this isolated wilderness was a heaven-sent gift. As soon as the day's tsetse work was done, by about 2 p.m., when the labour gang put off their heavy brass three-gallon insecticide sprayers, which they'd cheerfully borne almost non-stop for seven hours, and retired to their own camp, he, more often than not, would forgo lunch and devote the remaining hours of daylight to watching and photographing the birds. He never tired of exploring the 'fadamas' – wide, grassy meadows completely flooded in the wet season and even now, still marshy; the pools and lakes, still shallow at this time of year, offered miles of open water for a glorious array of birds. On our first day with him we saw more than fifty species, many rare, ranging from tiny sandpipers and lesser lily-trotters who daintily tread the carpet of wide leaves and search for insects among the blossoms, to great grey pelicans lumbering through the sky like early aeroplanes, then diving together as at a given signal, their bodies suddenly streamlined as if transformed by magic into creatures of the underwater world.

This was 'safari' as I'd always imagined it.

The camp was in untouched forest and we sat in the cool, dappled shade of the overhead canopy, marvelling and listening intently to the rustlings and occasional splashings of this secret world. Philip had put up a large, green tent for our use and at night, for the first time since reaching Nigeria, we snuggled under blankets and slept in comfort.

In the early morning we drove in Philip's battered truck to see the spraying in progress. I hoped we would arrive in time to hear the overseer's first command, 'Agoya! Agoya!' which means 'Carry your babies!' – as their wives do with their picans on their backs – so the men hoist up the heavy brass sprayers or the refill cans before beginning their long stint, working in pairs. However, we were delayed by our encounter with a hunter, wizened but wiry, a large warthog almost dwarfing him slung across his shoulders, bow and arrows in hand. Philip stopped the truck. A bargain was struck and the man hacked off a great bloody leg with the panga he kept stuck in his belt, and to general satisfaction, the day's menu was settled.

The 'work inspection' over, Philip had much to show us, and soon we alighted beside a wide pool which was starred with cream-and-crimson water lilies. He pointed out a fish eagle soaring high above us, and lesser-banded harriers circling as they watched for unwary prey. Among the lily leaves were tiny pygmy geese, almost invisible despite their bright colours, and around the water's edge hovered dozens of pied kingfishers.

Of course there was a price to pay for these riches in the shape of tormenting tsetses, as well as *Simulium damnosum* – aptly named as it's the most voracious and troublesome fly, the vector of the parasite causing river blindness, which can afflict whole village populations.

Almost a whole day was spent tramping and paddling round the fringes of a great fadama where enormous herds of Fulani cattle were coming in to graze, despite the spraying programme being not yet complete. Flocks of guinea fowl scattered on our approach, an easy target for the men, although they seemed instinctively to know when *I* held the gun and dodged my excited aim.

On the wide stretches of shallow water, spangled with purple lilies, were hundreds upon hundreds of waterfowl. There were geese and duck in infinite variety besides tall herons, gangly storks, spectacular crowned cranes and graceful sacred ibis.

My shooting skill suddenly improved and to all our amazement a large spurwing goose fell out of the sky at my feet. Beginners' luck, the men were quick to point out. The large flocks of pintail, garganey and 'wishi' – wood ducks – offered tempting targets and each man quickly bagged a couple of birds, but their triumphant smiles faded when one that Philip had winged refused to admit defeat. It gamely led them a duck-and-dive dance through acres of knee-deep water until a passing herdsman intervened and retrieved it easily. Exhausted and relieved, they cheerfully rewarded him with the bird and he went off chuckling to himself while they examined their legs for leeches. Philip carried a supply of disinfectant around, just in case of bilharzia, and they swabbed themselves optimistically.

Surveying our trophies, we decided Peter's knobnose goose should provide the evening's feast, Philip's team should have three of the other birds, and my prize spurwing be saved for tomorrow. 'And we'll have Nile perch for breakfast,' added our host.

Before returning to camp, Philip provided us with yet another fascinating insight into the secrets of this magical world. In some of the deep hoofprints left in the mud by the grazing cattle, we saw, with the aid of binoculars, tiny, perky birds – immigrant pipits from the far north – sheltering in the deep, cool hollows, not only from the sun, but also from the rapacious gaze of the lanner falcon, scrutinizing the ground from above. This bird could plummet from the sky quicker than a blink and would snatch one of the crowd of yellow wagtails, also innocently enjoying the wide expanse of churned-up mud.

There was just time before sundown for a walk beside the 'river' alongside the camp, where we watched for bulging eyes and log-like shapes drifting through the water. A rustle in a nearby thicket warned us to keep stock still as a family of warthogs emerged and stepped daintily down to the water's edge to drink. Our scent must have betrayed us, as mother lifted her head within seconds and, as if at a silent command, they all turned and trotted swiftly back into the shelter of thick bush, their little tails held high and straight like children's flags in a procession.

The bank was littered with oyster and mussel shells which the big 'open bills' had emptied and left behind. To our right we saw an eagle drop like a stone into a tree top and emerge, seconds later,with a long wriggling snake imprisoned in its fierce beak and talons.

The following day we drove to a fadama, new even to Philip, which was still covered in a couple of feet of swamp water, so was ungrazed, untouched and lay lush under the scorching sun. There was a tall, ugly marabou standing knee-deep in the water, filling up the pendulous pink globe that hangs like an enormous dewlap under his neck.

To attract the kingfishers that abounded, but had no place to perch actually over the water, Philip produced a sturdy branch which he drove into the soft mud at the edge. Almost immediately, when we had withdrawn, the first bird bagged its place, and I soon saw why it would be useful to this particular species – the pied variety – who need a convenient spot where they can deal with fish too large to swallow in flight: *sinodontis* is a favourite dish, but protects itself with long sharp spines that the kingfisher has to manoeuvre carefully in order to break.

The thick long grass made it difficult to see the bird life on one short visit, but it was there, in all its rich variety, and in full view there were three magnificent herons, larger than any we had seen previously. Philip almost exploded with excitement. 'Goliaths!' he breathed incredulously. 'Now there's something I never expected to see!' Taking no notice of us, the giant birds stalked slowly about the shallow water, stabbing through the matted grass under their feet to impale unwary mudfish.

On our last day, while Peter went off with the spray team, Philip and I strolled once more beside the old water-course in the early morning: as he said, it was like a busy street, so full of variety and bustling life. My pleasure in the now-familiar scene was tinged with sadness as I realised there was no chance of ever returning to this unspoiled Eden, remote and almost inaccessible, despite its size of about 200 square miles: a unique oasis in a land of semi-desert bordering the Sahara.

Two hours later Peter was back and we were away. As we emerged from the deep shadows of luxuriant foliage into the monotonous tedium of the open plain, it was as if we had enjoyed a performance in a living theatre and come out at the end of the play on to an empty road. As the heat and glare closed in on us I was forced to shut my eyes against the relentless oscillation of the vibrating air, and the painful realisation hit me that the curtain would soon come down for the very last time; the untouched Arcadia which we had been privileged to glimpse would shortly be despoiled once the guardian of its secret treasures – the tsetse fly – had been vanquished.

The gloom of such thoughts was deepened by the certainty (probably quite illogical) that, despite the vastness of this transequatorial region, Africa was inexorably tightening her grip on us. The past few days had been an easing of tension, not liberation. Feeling myself drifting back into lethargy, I wondered if I, like the catfish which, deprived of water for months, enters a state of aestivation, could suspend my own animation, until revived by a cool Cotswold breeze?

Such meanderings were swiftly smothered when Peter said, 'We'll have to start packing for the move to Gombe the minute we get back ......'

Birds of Sarbo
Left: Red-throated bee-eater
Right: Knob-billed goose

Below left: Goliath heron
Below right: Night heron

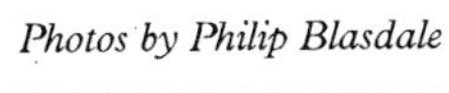

Photos by Philip Blasdale

CHAPTER 6

Two days of frantic packing followed our return from Phil's camp, then we bounced over 90-odd miles of corrugations to the cotton-growing centre, Gombe.

The Yard superintendent, a side-burned smooth-talking cockney, part of whose job it was to prepare accommodation for incoming officers, was glibly reassuring about our 'lovely, lovely little 'ouse ... bes' view on the station 'n all that ... all painted up, too'.

Following his directions we looked hopefully for what might pass for a hill with a house on top, but the nearest to this description was a shallow, rocky slope a couple of hundred yards beyond the dingy Clubhouse.

Surely that little rabbit hutch of a place couldn't be it? My heart sank. A line of four small rooms fronted by a frowning verandah under a corrugated iron roof stood in a barren compound, lifeless except for one straggly bougainvillea beside the house. A dozen noisy goats retreated a few yards, then turned to survey us curiously as Peter struggled to unlock the door.

One glance inside was enough. There was no way we could, or would, move in today. Annoyed and despondent we went to find the local Rest House.

Shade temperature of 100° is not an ideal condition for hard slog, but we all had to knuckle down to it. However, no matter how we scrubbed and polished the shabbiness of the furniture remained; ink stains, scratches, discolouration and wide cracks laughed at our efforts. The resident colony of lizards made no attempt to move to other quarters and chased each other round the walls and over the chairs as if to show us up as intruders.

In defence of the Yard Superintendent, I admit there had been an attempt at re-decoration but most of the walls had been painted a ghastly, livid peachy-pink and here we were in the throes of the hot season. Ironically, the smaller bedroom was, more appropriately, a cool blue-green, but was unusable as it was completely bare. Not even a bed.

The mattresses in the main bedroom were stained, smelly and filthy, but it took so long to persuade the Yard Superintendent to replace them that we decided our camp beds would be preferable. The house was like an oven, even at night, but there was a funny little 'room' with mesh walls like a large animal's cage tacked on to the side, which offered the best chance of relative coolness, so we slept there. We had to bend low and creep swiftly to the beds by torchlight for fear of being seen from the Club House – only a slight possibility, but one which made me feel uncomfortable nonetheless, and meant staying under a sheet, however steamy the night.

The station had little to recommend it. The Club appeared to be not only 'MEN ONLY' but 'US ONLY', and none of the ginnery workers, who seemed to spend all their free time there, ever spoke to us.

We tried playing tennis, but the court had been so neglected, the bumps and potholes made it dangerous as well as useless.

Easter in such surroundings seemed very strange. It is of course not celebrated by Muslims, and we marked the holiday by driving south about forty miles to Tula. For most of the way the land remained stubbornly jaundiced, but knobby hills began to appear, and soon we saw laboriously-made terraces on jutting rocks where little walls built of thousands of small hand-broken stones formed protective pockets of soil for cultivation.

Above the terraces were tight clusters of little mud huts, hundreds of them, packed closely together. This relatively small area supports 60,000 primitive people, pagans, whose only concession to modesty is a bunch of leaves fore and aft. They are famous for their pottery skills and their beautifully ornamented vessels are in contrast to the ubiquitous calabash – a large hollowed-out gourd which grows on vines.

Next day we discovered the price of driving on these horrendous roads: the cross-member of our new car (sole support of engine and gearbox) was badly cracked. The manufacturer's guarantee was useless and we were 350 miles from the garage. To our relief, a mechanic at the N. A. Yard was able to do a good welding job, and we breathed again.

In Gombe we were able to see how 'town houses' in the North are constructed. River clay, called 'banco' is mixed with straw and moulded round a simple scaffolding of branches, with the ends sticking out for ease of applying future coats, done after every rainy season.

Several streets (all unpaved) had rickety shacks and stalls clustered together to form markets, which spill over into whatever space is available, and stallholders sell spices, condiments, 'magic' potions, grain, lengths of cloth, as well as fruit and vegetables and sacks of groundnuts.

The sight of food must be a considerable trial during the month of Ramadan, when fasting must be observed between dawn and nightfall. The period ends with a great celebration, Sallah, which is so important an event that you would expect it to be precisely marked in the calendar. Not so. It officially begins 'when the new moon rises', but this may or may not be seen all over the country simultaneously. The night may be cloudy, the watchers over-anxious or deluded by optimism. On this occasion, conflicting reports raged around Gombe over two days – and in the confusion, no work was done. The Emir refused to accept the assurances of five moon-viewers appointed in outlying districts to inform him (a minimum of three sightings is required) and called them to his palace to report to him personally.

Flowers of the Sahel

Above: Frangipani

Right: Desert Rose

Below: Cocolospermum

Celebrating Sallah at the Emir's Palace in Gombe
Photograph by Philip Blasdale

Still unconvinced, he announced he would wait and see the moon rise for himself and at last, at 6.15pm, he and we were rewarded by the sight of the finest, most delicate crescent of silver thread gliding into view above the rose-pink glow of the dying sun.

Great rejoicing in Gombe. Sallah had begun.

❧❧❧❧

By custom, European government officers and their families were invited to the Emir's palace on the occasion of the durbar held to celebrate Sallah, so a handful of us were escorted up the steps to the tower above the gateway which opened on to the wide courtyard, giving us a bird's eye view of the colourful scene. What medieval splendour! Even though attendance by a number of chiefs from outlying districts had been forbidden by the Emir, owing to an outbreak of meningitis, the crush of crowds lining the streets was so dense that the narrow gap down the middle had to be forcibly widened by the police. All were in their best robes, snow-white and immaculate, while the women of the Emiral household gathered shyly in the passage leading from their quarters to the great portal, self-conscious in their rich brocades, gleaming gold and emerald. There were scores of them, some matronly, others handsome young women, or even giggling teenage girls. Most of them were struggling to hold in check one or two lively little picans.

After a splendidly British parade of the Northern Police in smart red and navy uniforms, complete with brass band, the great gathering of chiefs began.

The Emir waited, motionless, at the gate of the palace on his noble white horse, a most impressive figure, richly arrayed in many-layered robes of shimmering purple and wearing an immense turban, while two bare-headed attendants held a giant parasol, richly draped, over his head. An old greybeard, whom one sensed had had long and close association with him, fanned the Emir constantly and with great solicitude. Two bored but docile camels with swaying, supercilious heads stood immediately behind the royal personage, their backs each supporting a great leather drum, upon which was pounded out a monotonous, unchanging rhythm.

Now the chiefs were ready, also proudly mounted and resplendent in gorgeous bunched-up satins of glittering hues, with so many layers I couldn't imagine how it was possible to endure the heat. Their feet and legs were encased in long, leather stirrups like over-boots, and on top of their indigo turbans – shining after the cloth had been beaten for days with wooden poles – they wore plumed helmets like knights of old. This impression was strengthened by the sight of bright chain-mail vests worn by several of them ('Manufactured in Birmingham,' someone whispered in my ear!).

They collected together in clusters of about a dozen, two or three hundred yards from their overlord, then, at a signal, kicked their steeds into a lightning gallop and raced pell-mell towards him, spears raised like lances, to be hurled into the ground as they halted abruptly in front of him. This, the 'Jafi', symbolised their loyalty to their feudal ruler.

The ceremony of homage continued for an hour, enlivened at intervals by the antics of the 'Court Jester', who appeared to take precedence over everyone, even the magisterial elders, as he pranced around in his eye-catching leopard-skin robes and enormous head-dress.

We regretted not being able to understand his sallies, but our attention was suddenly distracted by a commotion in the crowd as, during the last of the charges, one of the horses appeared to stumble, unseating his princely rider, who fell inelegantly on to the dusty road, knocking his turban and helmet awry, but fortunately not seeming to suffer serious hurt – except, no doubt, to his pride. I imagine he was protected by his voluminous costume, which must have cushioned the impact considerably.

No official notice was taken of this small disaster and the chiefs followed their lord into the palace for further celebrations, while the townspeople dispersed to continue their own, less inhibited festivities, which went on all day and night.

❧❧❧❧

April's heat continued to intensify as the annual rainy season approached and the humidity made life almost unbearable. How we envied the 'commercial types' whose companies ensured that every possible civilised convenience was made available to them! We had heard that some even had air-conditioning.

Our sole relief was from getting into the bath several times a day. Water was only available between 9 p.m. and 6 a.m., so it was vital to fill all available containers during the night. Ignoring the fact that it looked exactly like Heinz tomato soup, and that when we emerged after a few minutes blessed coolness, the towels were stained red and our clothes felt as if they had come straight from under an iron, we shamelessly bathed in the same water over and over again.

For several weeks there was, almost daily, a tantalising build-up of storm clouds, piling up on every quarter of the horizon, advancing until almost overhead, only to turn tail in the face of an exasperatingly fickle wind, leaving us perspiring and limp. Meanwhile, there were reports of rain in every other part of Nigeria, except the furthest north.

One day was particularly oppressive and by late afternoon we could see the flashing of electric storms all around us and dark curtains of rain perhaps three or four miles distant in every direction. Holding our breath, we watched as the ink-black clouds drew closer, came right overhead, then suddenly split apart, as if axed, leaving a fissure of blue sky immediately above Gombe. There it remained for a further three hours, and we stood outside with the smell of wet earth in our nostrils, but the ground beneath our feet iron-hard and dry. Streaks of lightning dramatically illuminated the landscape, from blackest night into lurid daylight. The thunder rolled deafeningly, the wind howled round us, but still no rain fell on Gombe.

Marabou storks

Pelicans in the Sarbo

West African crowned cranes

Photography by Philip Blasdale

Sabon gari (market place) in Kaduna

Our rumfa surrounded by fire

Then a brief miracle. The faint patch above our heads disappeared and a sharp rattling on the roof announced that the rains, if not yet arrived, were on their way.

Now we had to keep a sharp lookout for scorpions which prefer the shelter of a house in the rainy season, so shoes and slippers had to be carefully shaken out and it was unwise to go barefoot, especially after dark. Snakes, too, were more in evidence. A six-foot cast skin by our kitchen door made us scour the compound for its erstwhile owner, and Peter, suspecting the hole under a large rock, poured petrol down and threw in a lighted match. The explosion sent the rock a foot into the air, and while there was no sign of the occupant, a big cobra with a beautifully shiny skin was seen heading out towards the Clubhouse later that day.

As the rains continued their hiccupping approach, bare shrubs in the compound began optimistically to sprout, but the goats returned en-masse, quickly devouring anything remotely green. We were astounded to see them standing on their hind legs, pulling branches down with their forelegs. They even climbed an old, wide-rooting tree with low projecting branches which they jumped on to reach juicy-looking leaves, or to escape the randy billies' attentions! The pervasive smell and the blaring bleats added to our exasperation with these unwelcome visitors. The one pleasurable feature of the 'garden' was the old tree, a large fig, which hid a fantastic variety of bird life; mostly tiny creatures, no bigger that your thumb, gaily colourful and busy, who shared their home with several pairs of green pigeons with wings of bright emerald and breasts of brilliant yellow. Their song is remarkable, a sequence of softly repeated, gradually descending notes.

❧❧❧❧

Despite the stupefying heat, survey work was even more urgent now that the dry season was coming to an end, and as a wide area around a string of small lakes, called the Matyoro, was to be prepared ready for a big fly-eradication scheme after the rains, Peter proposed we should camp there for a few weeks. Although only thirty-odd miles away, the trip would not be easy. He and his team had already tried to follow the single cattle trail through untouched bush on bicycles and had been defeated by the treacherously soft, sandy track. Now he had to transport men and equipment in the big five-ton lorry and would have to take the wheel himself as the African driver couldn't cope in such difficult conditions.

Planning a very early start, our first frustration was finding that Maman and Dalmia had forgotten to boil and filter water in readiness. There was enough in the fridge to fill one thermos and we took another three to fill when we reached the lakes. Unfortunately, during the packing of the car for the first stage of the journey, Dalmia dropped the precious full flask, leaving us with none.

There was no time to boil more, and in any case our firewood store was suddenly and suspiciously empty.

Peter had arranged to arrive at Gadam, the last settlement before the vast, uninhabited area – which the Department hoped would ultimately be safe for human re-settlement – before the lorry, and during the half-hour wait for it, the villagers crowded round the car, curious to catch sight of white skin, especially that of a woman. Peter climbed out of the car to greet the Sarkin, or chief, and elders, and the men-folk clustered round to hear the discussion, interpreted by Mallam Isa, the leader of Peter's team, while I, smiling but dumb, sat surrounded by mothers with babies at their breasts and round-eyed, pot-bellied picans shyly peeping out from behind them.

The lorry arrived and everything was transferred into it, the car to be left in the care of the Sarkin. A dozen men squeezed into the back alongside the equipment and our baggage. Peter took the wheel and we bumped and swayed through the narrow village alleys, barely missing the flimsy straw-matting huts. We emerged to tackle the tiny path, not two feet across, over brown stubble which, within a hundred yards, gave way to continuous bush, where the path had been widened by hacking down the more substantial trees on either side.

It was now past midday and the cab was like a furnace. The sun's fierce reflected glare forced me to keep my eyes turned away from the bonnet.

At first the main danger was of the tyres being slashed by the sharp stumps concealed in the undergrowth, and progress was slow, but Peter negotiated the now frequent patches of deep sand with such skill that there seemed no cause for worry. He was pleased that we'd covered four miles in two-and-a-half hours.

Now the heat was getting unbearable. It was impossible to move one's legs without burning them on hot metal. At this point the track sloped downward into a deep bed of sand. The engine juddered and stalled. The men climbed down and, with sweat pouring off their bodies, tried to push the lorry forward.

I tried to ignore the desperate thirst that suddenly seemed so much worse, as I watched the men straining with superhuman effort. The truck moved forward slightly, then sank even deeper into the sand. Even Peter was losing his customary calm and was quietly cursing the Department's Admin. Officer for insisting, against all advice, that he use such a heavy vehicle for his 'bush-whacking'.

Pangas (slashers) were unloaded and the men set about hacking down branches and saplings which they spread in front of the wheels for about thirty yards over a track they'd dug out to reach what seemed to be firmer ground.

As we climbed back into the cab, searing pain flashed across my legs as I accidentally brushed against the gearbox. The lorry lurched and heaved, achieved a few yards, then sank again. The same body-wrenching efforts by the men eventually moved us a yard or two, but then down we went. Like a faulty slide-projector continually clicking up the same picture, the scene was repeated over and over again.

I felt panic rising in my dry throat. The cab with its white-hot sides, seemed to be closing in on me. It was painfully difficult to keep my feet down, as the heat from below forced its way up through my flimsy sandals, but there was nowhere else I could put them. I sat in a pool of sweat, my dress sodden. Peter

Our home at Ririwai

Rumfa – de luxe model

Birds of Sarbo

Top left: Fish eagle
Top right: Carmine bee-eater

Below left: Hadada ibis
Below right: African darter

Photography by Philip Blasdale

helped me climb out again, and it clung wetly to the back of my legs. He called to Mallam Isa and they disappeared to confer, while I looked in vain for a patch of shade where I could find relief from the merciless sun. There was none. The featureless, flat scrub stretched mockingly, endlessly, in every direction; not a bird sang; not a lizard stirred. It was as if the land lay paralysed in the stupefying heat. It felt as if I, too, were being suffocated.

Just as terror seemed to be overwhelming me, Peter appeared, a small cup of water in his hand, and I sipped, thankfully. Mallam Isa roused the exhausted men to yet more effort and somehow, after a further hour of curses, prayers and sweating struggle, the lorry was forced round to face the way we'd so painfully come, and fresh branches laid for forty or fifty yards.

By now, scarcely two hours of daylight remained, yet the heat still simmered unrelentingly. The engine throbbed into life as the men climbed wearily into the back and I lowered myself gingerly on to a towel spread over the burning leather of the seat.

For a few agonising seconds we sensed the wheels threatening to return to helpless spinning, but at last they gripped. Slowly the truck was forced upwards, then remained for a couple of seconds miraculously balanced on the first log. There was a sudden lurch, we toppled forwards and the momentum carried us on in slow, drunken progress like a small boat in a stormy sea, battering, jolting and hurling its crew in all directions.

As if melting in its own heat, the sun was rapidly vanishing as the cluster of Gadam's huts came into view, and by the time the lorry rumbled to a stop in the market area, night had fallen.

Reaching our house in Gombe, I was too exhausted to eat, or even wash off the red, grimy dust of the day. I stumbled under the mosquito net and went straight to sleep.... But not for very long. Two hours later, another nightmare began and my body was gripped by raking claws that tore my stomach apart. I lay doubled-up on clammy sheets, drenched with sweat, unable to move, scarcely able to cry out for the intensity of the pain.

Peter carried me to the bathroom where a torrent of blood surged out of my body, but still leaving me racked with pain and fear.

At dawn he slipped out of the house and at last I slept. A strange figure was bending over me when I woke.

'Sorry, sorry, sorry,' Dr Wernik was saying. 'No more baby now.' Rest two or three days I think. And next time, no trips to the bush, eh?'

CHAPTER 7

As soon as I was well enough to be left, Peter set off again for the Matyoro lakes on a foot safari with a team of labourers to begin the task of building roads – or at least usable tracks – in preparation for the detailed survey and for the spraying operations which would begin sometime in the following dry season.

He returned to find me in despair. It appeared that someone had broken into the kitchen during the night and stolen a pile of my clothes, as well as our remaining good bed linen – all were awaiting ironing. Dalmia seemed to be very upset and said he had heard nothing, but when Peter took a closer look at the kitchen, he realised that all the glass had fallen outside the window, so whoever broke it must have done so from the inside.

Confronted with this evidence, and angrily accused by Maman, who had been on tour with Peter, Dalmia had no answer. The local police were called and the boy taken away for questioning.

For three weeks we heard nothing, and there was no sign of the stolen goods, to my great exasperation as the clothes had all been bought in the UK and I knew I couldn't replace them here. There was also the problem of finding someone reliable to replace Dalmia.

As it was essential for the cook to accompany Peter on his tours, it was a relief to have a young man of about twenty recommended to us as steward. Mohammedu was from Biu, and we knew that servants from that area had an excellent reputation. He was quiet, sensible and a paragon compared to Dalmia.

Finally, a letter arrived from the police sergeant. It said, 'Dear Sir, This boy Dalmia Ako, swear on the Bible, he no be guilty of this thing. He be good Christian boy and God will forgive him. He is telling this and we let him go free. Your Obedient Servant...'

The very next morning, we were amazed to find Dalmia himself on the doorstep, expecting his job back! With a wide smile he admitted the theft, but said it did not matter because 'me be good Christian and bad things He always forgive me'. I'm afraid Peter sent him away with a flea in his ear. We were particularly annoyed that he could not or would not tell us where the things were now. Just shrugged and smiled.

The long wait for the rains continued, with tempers short and very minor irritations seeming an insufferable burden. One afternoon, as we looked longingly at the dark, cloud-wrapped horizon, we became conscious of a distant roaring which magnified as a leaden mantle overwhelmed the space all round us, blotting out the town entirely. Suddenly we found ourselves swept off our feet by a stinging, gritty blast. The grey sheets curtaining Gombe were not deluging rain, but storm winds of thick dust which sent us running into the house to batten down doors and windows. The smell of rain was strong in our nostrils, but the dust storm lasted so long we began to doubt if it would ever reach us.

Bargaining with door-to-door salesmen in Kaduna

Road-making on the project

Eventually it came, in the form of a brief shower, but then the clouds departed, far more swiftly than they'd arrived, leaving us limp and disappointed.

Our spirits received another blow when, shortly after setting out towards Bauchi to renew depleted stores, an ominous noise from under the car led to the discovery that, once again, the cross-member had fractured.

Limping back to Gombe, we discovered that the town's only welding machine had broken down. Only a make-do repair was possible.

Next day we managed to reach Bauchi, but the mechanical engineer there refused to touch it. 'There's a grave likelihood of severe damage to the gears. It's been driven a hundred miles with engine and gearbox out of alignment.'

With fingers crossed, we set out for Jos and were enormously relieved to arrive. The garage mechanic there assured us it could be done ... but at the end of the day three attempts had been made to repair it, and the car was in a worse condition than before.

We stayed at the Jos Club, the Rest House being full, and returned to the garage the next morning. There we sat, all day, while the cross-member was removed, re-ground and re-welded, a further *four* times. It was 4.15 p.m. when we finally left Jos to return via Bauchi to Gombe.

Peter had also asked that a faulty shock absorber be checked, but at 10p.m., still 30 miles from Gombe, and 170 miles from the garage in Jos, a sudden loud banging from the back of the car told us the worst. Crawling underneath with a torch, Peter discovered the inevitable – the mechanic had removed the *good* shock absorber and left the faulty one. Peter tied the offender up with a piece of string and we crawled anxiously home.

These difficulties meant further delays in completing the survey, which had somehow to be finished before the rains set in, when we were due to move to Kaduna. We'd already had a preview of the chaos they would bring. After a storm of only a couple of hours one morning, the Bauchi road was transformed into a torrent swirling in front of us, having washed away large chunks of the road. There were now rivers four or five feet deep on either side, and the force of water had shattered stone culverts – this with the first rain for more than seven months.

As we sat pondering the situation, an impatient, and presumably inexperienced, European driver of a Land Rover put his foot down hard and tried to get through at top speed. It was easy to see from the dozens of Africans wading in the flood that under the surface there were deep ruts of two feet or so. The vehicle hit one, leapt six feet in the air, throwing out two men in the back who were lucky to survive, and landed on its side.

A 'mammy-wagon' driver tried the same approach. The huge vehicle came to a shuddering, juddering halt, and leaned dangerously over as we sidled past.

Our lives were cheered up by the arrival of a little grey kitten, who, despite her insistence on leaving large puddles in unsuitable places (beds and armchairs were her favourites), quickly became an indispensable part of the household.

Now that there were occasional night-time storms, we were driven indoors to the one usable bedroom from our 'camp cage' and there at six every morning the fun began.

One double-size mosquito net covered the two beds and somehow 'Louise' managed to leap on top of it and run about over our heads to let us know it was time for her to be let in too. As soon as we did so, she leapt into action, furiously attacking fingers and toes, stampeding over us and hurling herself, teeth bared in mock fury, at our sensitive extremities.

Having reduced us to helpless hysteria, she would turn her attention to the net, itself a marvellous thing to swing on, hooking her claws in to rip out teeny holes. She was incorrigible and I spent many mornings darning up the damage.

A family of hawks was nesting in a tree near the house, and we watched, fascinated, as the parent birds cajoled and coaxed the youngsters in order to get them to venture off the branch. They called to each other constantly, the one timid and imploring, the other encouraging and persuasive. All intruders – storks, vultures, big pied crows – were seen off when they attempted to gatecrash.

The patience of the parents was a marvel. One sat on the branch of a nearby tree for an unbroken twenty-four hours, except for brief forays for food which it brought to its frightened offspring who was refusing to budge more than two feet from the nest. If a youngster got into real difficulty, as happened quite often, the adult would fly to its side and remain there, reassuringly, until danger was past, or the fledgling had extricated itself.

Another fascination was the private life of lizards. We watched, on several occasions, when a 'mother-to-be' dug a sizeable, vertically-sided hole, so deep that only her tail was visible as, completely 'end-up', she completed her preparations. Every few seconds she surfaced and looked warily about and above her for two or three minutes at a time, before finally sitting over the cavity in an attitude of intense concentration and laying, at intervals of a minute or so, eight snow-white eggs. With the same care as before, she covered them with the sandy soil piled in readiness, dragging her tail over the surface to level it and make it indistinguishable from the surrounding area. The whole process from start to finish took over an hour.

The nuisance of thousands more insects invading our lives was mitigated somewhat by studying them. Hordes of flying ants zoomed into the lounge in the evening, and Peter, a keen observer and a fund of information, pointed out that they shed their wings the moment they land and are then an easy prey to any predator. To some East African tribes they are a delicacy: apparently they taste like porridge. At twilight we found the spot in the compound where they emerged – three holes in the ground where thousands, still in the 'grub' stage, were milling round the narrow exits where adults pushed their way through, whirred new wings – to be used for only half an hour, perhaps, before being discarded – and flew off. Just like planes emerging at speed from crowded hangars.

Close to the nests was another of Nature's small wonders, so perfectly camouflaged that Peter's keen eyes only just spotted it, and it was with great difficulty that I eventually made it out. What looked like an ordinary tiny stone was in fact the lid of the den of the 'trapdoor spider'. He remains quite hidden until an unwary insect walks by, then *woof*! The lid opens just a fraction and a hairy arm shoots out ...

As rainstorms became more frequent, the countryside was transformed. In spite of the intense heat, the tender new foliage massing on the trees and the emerald carpet now covering the sandy wastes gave an impression of spring, strengthened by the appearance – within hours of a rainfall – of beautiful yellow flowers growing in clusters, exactly like primroses. These are *cocolospermum* (see page 30) and they never ceased to amaze and enchant me, materialising as they did out of seemingly barren ground.

Even the garden, neglected and goat-ravaged, glowed with unexpected colour. Vying with the purple bouganvillea, with its apparently immortal flowers, although leaves only appeared with the rains, was the exotic 'flamboyant tree', aptly named for its fiery scarlet blooms. Shrubs we'd imagined to be quite dead burst into blossom and defeating the daily onslaught of the goats became a priority.

As soon as the soil is softened, peasant farmers begin planting, though there's little in the way of 'cultivation'. The seed, dropped by hand, is trodden down firmly. All that remains is to wait five months, when the sorghum or millet will be ready to harvest.

Now we had the occasional pleasure of waking in the morning to grey skies and an insistent pattering on the roof. Torrential downpours were becoming frequent, usually preceded by violent winds and dust storms. At night there was sometimes so much lightning that it seemed as if it was the blackness interrupting the startling incandescence. Once, just after midnight, the whole plain stretching away from the back of our 'hill' was illuminated without interruption for over an hour before the cloak of darkness descended again. The bougainvillea blooms glowed crimson and purple amongst their newly sprouted leaves and it was nearly 2 o'clock before 'night' returned.

CHAPTER 8

The customary confusion surrounded arrangements for our move to Kaduna for the bulk of the rainy season. Instructions from HQ consisted solely of the date of departure. No mention of accommodation or the means by which we might transport our worldly goods. At the same time we received a letter from complete strangers thanking us for agreeing to host their stay in the capital during the week of celebration for Nigeria's independence. Who and where were these people?

Contrary to our previous impressions of Gombe, the town suddenly looked lively and attractive. With the advent of the rains it woke up from its long sleep and buzzed with activity. The big shady trees lining the streets burst into blooms of dazzling scarlet, like the one beside our compound, and we watched at sundown as hundreds of white ibis crowded on those around the Emir's palace. They clustered so thickly that the branches looked snow-mantled, a soft blizzard of feathers filling the air as they jostled for the best perch, in undignified uproar at odds with their elegant appearance.

There was no time to savour these unexpected delights. Only a week remained for Peter to tie up the ends of his survey and for preparations to be made for the move. At last the news of where we were actually to live percolated through and it was far better than we had hoped for, at first sight. We were to 'sit in' the Director's house while he was on leave, which might be for three or four months.

We arrived to find a rambling, creeper-covered ranch-house offering space and furnishing – luxurious after our Gombe experience. There were even two bathrooms, a normal water supply and, to my great joy, electricity.

The garden – a real one, not a bare compound – was nearly two acres of lawn, flower beds, shrubs and shady trees. There were plants I hadn't expected to see in West Africa – hollyhocks, dahlias and roses for example, as well as great clumps of flame-coloured canna lilies. Hedges of sky-blue plumbago bordered the path from the front door leading to shady walks under the satiny-white, headily-scented blooms of frangipani, beside purple oleander, scarlet hibiscus and, beneath, wonderful buttercup-yellow allamandas and masses of bougainvillea adorning trellises and the house itself.

Our beautiful surroundings were some compensation for the difficulties that were about to cloud our horizon.

The head of the Tsetse Unit, acting in Dr Wilson's absence, instructed Peter to continue surveying throughout the rainy season, in an area some hundred miles distant, which meant that he would be 'on tour' for two weeks out of every three during months when most roads were impassable and any bush 'paths' would have vanished under twelve foot high grass. Trekking through the bush in prolonged tropical downpours and keeping dry in camp were not very practical propositions either, but M. refused to budge. He also ordered that work should not be interrupted by the four days' public holiday, which was to mark the country's step towards self-government. This was ludicrous, as none of the project team would be available that week.

M.'s attitude was puzzling, unpleasant and reeked of spite, which was quite inexplicable until a colleague at HQ whispered the reason. Apparently he was furious that Dr Wilson had personally recruited Peter, on contract, without consulting him, and he felt personally affronted. Peter was warned that enmity from that quarter could make life difficult – a prediction that was to be all too accurately fulfilled.

Other worries were financial. Despite the attractive terms of Peter's contract, the Administrative Department still had not got round to paying the huge expenses involved in carrying out this work. M., who could have pushed them, did not want to know.

Now we were dismayed to be sent a bill for the car we'd purchased on arrival in Kaduna for far more that the price quoted at the time, and without the discount of 5% we were entitled to. Studying the invoice, we discovered that, not only was the car an out-of-date model (which we'd have refused, had we known) but a note was added informing us that 'no complaints can be entertained after 14 days from the date of purchase'.

Standard Motors failed to reply to Peter's strongly-worded letter of protest, despite the fact that the disclaimer had been posted nearly five months after we'd bought the vehicle.

With Peter away for much of the time, our social life in Kaduna was non-existent. I longed to play tennis, but found that the Club rules made it impossible for any newcomer to play for months, unless they had an 'entrée' via some important member.

My efforts to find a job were stymied by the unreliability of the telephone, so I joined Peter on tour for a few days before the rains made travelling impossible. He had organised a camp in an abandoned mine company house: the roof looked likely to cave in at any moment, but it had four good walls and a wild, once lovely garden full of trees and rampantly flowering shrubs. The place was on the lower slopes of a range of small wooded hills, a refreshing change from the plain, and with mining activity moving away, some game was returning to the area. One evening we heard the cough of a leopard near the camp and next morning, Peter caught a glimpse of one disappearing into the dense scrub at first light. My only excitement came as we were driving along the narrow road to the camp: a lizard darted out of the grass and shot down the track in front of us, a large snake in hot pursuit. Both disappeared before we had recovered from our surprise, so I don't know which won the race.

A few miles into the hills, a mine was still operating, managed by an Englishman, whom we called on. We were introduced to his wife, a French girl in her twenties who was delighted with our company. I was the first white woman she had seen for eighteen months. She was not resentful of their isolation; a generator produced electricity for the house which was comfortably furnished and quite attractive, but they were having to prepare to return to Europe as she was expecting a baby, and the Company did not allow children to live at the mine with their parents.

Back in Kaduna, domestic problems were becoming pressing. The 'small boy' who had come with us from Gombe was unhappy and wanted to return – ostensibly because 'my brudder sick' – and we weren't sorry to lose him: the help he gave was non-existent, probably because Maman didn't teach him his duties. Mohammedu now always accompanied Peter on tour, so the cook did less and less. Meals were frequently inedible, and he seemed not to be capable of carrying out the simplest request. As Kaduna had electricity, we decided to get hold of a small cooker, so that I could cope in an emergency, but Maman's attempts to use it were disastrous. I discovered he kept it switched on high all afternoon for four hours before he began cooking in the evening. Then everything came out blackened and burnt.

A new 'garden boy' had been taken on by the Wilsons just before they went on leave. Unfortunately he had not been properly trained either. We left him with instructions to mow the lawn while we were away, and we returned to find he'd dug it up.

A bright new 'small boy' appeared at the door and we agreed to give him a trial, but within days Maman was accusing him of stealing: 'This boy Josa, him teef. No good small boy this'.

Having persuaded us that Josa shouldn't stay in the house, the very next day Maman announced his own departure. There was trouble with his wife in his home village. He had not wanted to bring her to Kaduna and now he presented Peter with a note:

'Sir, I wish report my wife to the Alkali court and for that I beg to let me go and watch her movement so that she should not part all my properties in the night and ran away.

Yours truly, Maman, Gombe'

Obviously he had engaged a scribe to write for him and, whether the story was true or not, we had no wish to keep him if he wanted to go. While we were both in Kaduna, we had the steward, Mohammedu to help us, but when Peter went away on tour, he had to take him. It was essential we find someone quickly. With power supplied and a comfortable house, I might have been able to manage alone, but without transport I could not reach the shops, and not knowing the language, I was unable to use the local market. The rains temporarily deserted us and the heat and humidity were intense. With no washing machine nor an electric iron, the laundry would have been impossible to cope with, especially as clothes often needed a complete change more than once a day.

In the midst of these worries, Peter developed a fever and rapidly became very ill. Weak after days of vomiting and with chest pains, he was admitted to hospital where he was left virtually unattended for 24 hours. When he was finally seen by a doctor, no diagnosis was made. 'Possibly food poisoning, though it could be dengue fever' was the first opinion. Two days later another doctor saw him: 'Malaria, I should think, or else virus pneumonia'.

He was sent home with a bottle of antibiotic pills, still weak but his strong constitution beginning to win through. Now, besides attending to preparations for the new survey, he found himself landed with administration duties at the Tsetse HQ.

It was a relief to find a reasonable replacement cook, another 'Maman' and a 'small boy' recommended by a departing ex-pat, so, as the domestic situation seemed settled, I applied for a teaching post at the Capital School in the town. This was for primary age children, those of professional and/or wealthy Nigerians as well as expatriates, though there were far fewer of the latter. I found myself taking a small class of seven and eight-year-olds, some of whom were the offspring of local emirs. Through contact with them, I began to have a small understanding of the home life of aristocratic Muslim families in Northern Nigeria.

At first it was puzzling that the children's potentially smart school uniforms were creased and grubby, except at the very beginning of term, until I discovered that small children stayed with their mothers, along with the other wives and concubines in the women's quarters – a cluster of small rooms quite separate from the grand house of their lord and master, and set around a courtyard where usually a fire was kept burning and where the children slept. Changing into pyjamas was a Western custom that had apparently not caught on here.

Much more concerning for me, a European living in a monogamous society, was the consequence of the vast number of children sired by one man, taking as many women and girls as he desired and could afford. (In the Gombe area we heard a gunfire salute for the seventieth son born to the emir. Girls were apparently not worth counting.)

The result of couplings between, say an eighty-year-old man and a twelve-year-old child may well be abnormal, and there were two such unfortunates in my class. One, Mohammedu, whom I couldn't resist calling in my own mind 'Jonathan Jo', had a long face and a mouth permanently open in the shape of a great O. The other, Abubakar, had widely-spaced eyes and a big grin that never left his face. He was hyperactive. Neither boy had normal intelligence and in other circumstances would have received specialist help.

As it was, there were difficulties enough with the Nigerian boys. Brought up to regard women – including their mothers – as inferior, no more than chattels, and themselves as junior despots, they acknowledged no authority other than their fathers' and behaved rudely and arrogantly towards women teachers. It took all my patience and firmness to impose a reasonable discipline in the classroom in order to create a harmonious atmosphere.

The little girls were entirely different. Like little mice, they spoke shyly, in whispers, if persuaded to speak at all. Trained from birth to be submissively obedient, it was hard to draw them out. There were far fewer of them, as not many fathers could be persuaded that their daughters were of sufficient importance to merit education. Even the daughter of the Sardauna, Sultan of Sokoto and the most important man in the region, had been confined to purdah and the women's quarters immediately on her return from the UK, where she had been educated at Cheltenham Ladies College, then won first class honours at Oxford.

Sad stories abounded about the fate of women and young girls forced into virtual slavery by their men-folk. A European nurse was called to the palatial compound of an emir in a distant part of the north, where she found in the stables more than a hundred young women who had been presented as tribute by lesser chiefs to their overlord. Presumably because there were more than he could accommodate, they were left there, in appalling conditions.

During our time in Kaduna, a little girl of twelve was taken to the main hospital, having swallowed the contents of a tin of Jeyes Fluid. She had been distraught at being sent to 'marry' an elderly man she'd never seen before, and had been forbidden to visit her mother and sisters. She died in agony.

I was lucky to have the distraction of work. Peter was away for most of the time and the rainy season became unexpectedly depressing with a succession of grey, drizzly days interspersed with spells of torrential rain. In the wardrobe, our clothes became stained with mildew and our shoes turned green; beds felt damp and when you laid your head on the pillow your nostrils filled with a mouldy stench impossible to ignore. But the temperature dropped and the insects became less troublesome.

Road conditions outside the town were frequently impossible, with bridges and culverts swept away and fords non-existent, particularly in the remote areas which Peter had to visit or survey.

A couple of weeks of violent afternoon storms foreshadowed the end of the wet season and the sunny mornings, fresh and clear, restored the spirits.

Uncertainty about the length of our tenure of Dr Wilson's house continued, as he changed his mind about his return date several times. At last a deadline for mid-October was set, so that would mark the end of my short spell at the Capital School.

Shortly before I left, an alarming incident occurred. During the lesson, a little Indian boy in my class glanced out of the open door and said, quite calmly, 'There's a snake coming, Mrs Aitchison'. I looked disbelievingly, but sure enough, a large greeny-brown snake between five and six feet long was heading straight for the step leading up to the classrooms. Hastily, but not feeling at all calm myself, I warned my colleague in the adjoining room to keep her door shut and the children inside, then shouted for the garden boy, who was nowhere to be seen. Fortunately at that moment the husband of one of the teachers drove up with a message for her. I shouted to him to stay in his car as he'd pulled up right beside it, a couple of feet from the step, and as soon as he saw it, he threw several heavy spanners at it, and the reptile was severely wounded. A Nigerian teacher, Mr Kolewole, hearing the commotion, came running out and finished it off. We were lucky, he said; it was a very dangerous one.

Our reprieve from having to move house in September gave us the chance to enjoy some of the fruit from the garden. There were lemons and mandarins, followed by oranges, pawpaw and guavas, which helped to compensate for the distasteful, never-ending tasks of sieving maggots out of flour, catching weevils which floated up out of breakfast cereals, and battling against armies of ants that managed to infiltrate even tightly-shut tins.

The senior 'garden boy', an exceptionally hard worker whom we feared was too good to be true, unfortunately proved us right. Mohammedu's wages, together with his riga (robe) were stolen from his quarters. Suli had taken them into the local township, sold the robe, then spent all the money on drink. He staggered back to the house, completely inebriated, and was found two days later sleeping it off under a shady tree at the far end of the garden. He was so full of remorse, we forgave him, but barely a week later he went off on the razzle all day. During his absence we discovered a newly-bought gin bottle of ours was almost empty, and several packets of Peter's cigarettes were missing. When he was sober enough to be tackled, he admitted his guilt and begged forgiveness, but we felt the Wilsons would not thank us for letting him continue, so he had to go.

A bout of malaria, heavy colds for both of us and my everlasting 'tummy palaver' made 'the little hot season' at the end of the rains very trying, especially as we had to prepare to move – never a straightforward matter.

We were assigned the house of a bachelor ex-pat who was supposed to have moved out and be staying at the local Rest House before returning to the UK. Peter arranged with him to take over at 11a.m., but there was no sign of him. Searching proved fruitless, and we seethed in the heat, waiting in the driveway for him to appear, which he finally did at almost five o'clock, without apology or explanation, handed over the key and drove off.

This was annoying enough, especially as we were expecting a colleague to stay the very next day, but worse was to come when the door was unlocked ... the place was a pigsty, and before we could begin to unpack, the whole house had to be scrubbed and polished. I suppose, being unmarried, he was unobservant where his surroundings were concerned, and his servants obviously were not about to enlighten him.

The curtains had been cut much too short and extra pieces tacked-on upside down, but that was a detail there was no time to attend to.

The house was a 'Muslim-type' and the rooms seemed very small and dark after our last house. There was a tiny garden and similar houses close by. The major snag was the proximity of a village, now that we were right on the edge of town, and that meant ceaseless drumming and wailing at night. I faced the prospect of being alone most of the time, with Peter away on the new scheme, and without transport or telephone, but that situation did not last very long, though it seemed we were going from the frying pan into the fire.

Within a matter of days, Peter was told we must quit the house and go and live 'on the scheme', where there was no accommodation at all. It was understandable that Dr Wilson was anxious that the scheme – a pilot – should be a success. If it was (i.e. cleared of tsetse during the coming year), a vast area known as Belt 27, covering thousands of square miles, would be tackled, the project financed by several million US dollars. But there was no consideration whatsoever shown to the man in charge.

Determined to have a little respite, we took a couple of days' local leave after packing up the Denham Road house and drove up to Kano, our only chance to visit before Peter was once again overwhelmed with work.

We were unprepared for the tremendous contrast with Kaduna, where the measured, spacious structure of its roads, European-style houses and impressive administrative buildings could have been lifted from a twentieth-century Western city and placed tidily in a central position in the savannah, and where Colonel Lugard had planned his peace-keeping strategy, bringing military efficiency to the colonial administration he established.

Kano on the other hand, is an ancient city, steeped in history. Thousands of little mud-baked houses crowd together higgledy-piggledy and of little permanence. Many are washed away, with tragic consequences, during the annual rains and we saw much ruin and debris, still uncleared after the havoc wreaked by violent storms the previous month. It was grim to contemplate the fate of families caught in a sea of mud.

The ancient city of Kano

We climbed up the steps to the top of one of the minarets of the principal mosque to enjoy a view of strange fantasy, the 'ears' of many little houses standing up like a crowd of rabbits. We were puzzled by the patchwork of small green squares spread all over the city. Not lawns, surely? Then we realised that all these mud roofs had sprouted grass during the rains and were covered with greensward which would shortly die off now that the rains were over.

For centuries Kano has been the centre of trade and manufacturing in the Western Sudan and a most important staging post on the caravan routes across the Sahara Desert.

We were struck by the sight of mammoth pyramids, most imposing until you realised that they were vast piles of groundnuts. The railway cannot cope with the prodigious quantity produced, Lagos having inadequate storage facilities to take the whole crop. There are also huge piles of sacks filled with millet and sorghum, the staple grains.

The city has long been famous for its cotton cloth, woven, embroidered, or dyed and treated to give it an extraordinary metallic sheen, like Lurex, but produced by a very elementary technique. We watched at the dye pits where muscular men, stripped to the waist, their bodies glistening with sweat, lifted out great lengths of indigo cloth and hung them over long poles stretched horizontally on waist-high racks. Then with heavy 'paddles' they beat the fabric until it developed the rich lustre required for royal robes.

We were amused by the names given to products sold in the many small drugstores: 'Lungo', 'Pylo', 'Spleeno', 'Rubbo' even 'Brayno', but we had to read the small print to discover that 'Moree' would 'ensure fertility'. 'Manpower' was pretty obvious, but we never did discover what 'Ho Ho' promised to do for you.

All the big market areas were noisy and full of vitality. We were besieged by traders crowding round us, crying 'Bature! Bature! (white men) Come see! Come see!'.

There was an abundance of leather goods, mostly goatskin but also camel and cowhide, tanning being a major industry here. Flashy jewellery and brilliantly hued scarves vied with thousands of mass-produced trashy goods imported from Birmingham. It was disappointing that there was a lack of good local crafts, but the colours, sounds and smells in the markets made a memorable experience. Later we found a store that seemed to have a monopoly of locally-made products, and we were able to buy good fabrics for curtains and bed-linen very cheaply.

A 'black spot' in our explorations was an area within the *sabon gari* (market area) where wild animals brought in by hunters or imported from nearby African countries were confined in appalling conditions, so bad that it was a wonder any survived to be sold on – presumably to zoos. It was too distressing to linger and there was nothing we could do.

Driving out from the city in the late afternoon, we found a greener landscape than expected, although it would not be many weeks before all growth withered and shrank to faded lifelessness again. A hill rose up not far from the city boundary, amazingly a concealed reservoir, the construction of which must have improved the lives of the citizens immeasurably. It is interesting that up until 1904, only a third of the area within the city walls, which encompassed more than seven square miles, was built on. Things changed when, at about that time, the British took control, and by 1906 the first road capable of carrying wheeled traffic to the coast was completed. In 1911 the railway reached Kano, and a vast expansion of trade began.

Not surprisingly, the Nigerian, like most Africans, spends most of his time outside rather than indoors, and we drove back as darkness fell through the narrow streets lit by tiny oil lamps illuminating prone figures, stretched out by doorways, squatting beside fires or scooping handfuls of highly spiced food from brightly coloured bowls.

For many, nothing had changed.

Refreshed after our short break, we returned to Kaduna only long enough to pack up and move out to 'bush' at Kari, some 130 miles away. For much of the time we lived in a 'rumfa', a temporary structure of straw matting supported on a rectangular framework of poles, where we were comparatively cool – a big relief in 'the little hot season' that follows the rains. About 35 miles distant was a partly-deserted mining camp at Ririwai, where a little box-like house was supposed to have been made ready for our use, but although someone had been in with a paintbrush, the furniture was mostly unusable. The place looked like a repair shop, with only the frames of the armchairs – just wooden arms and metal springs, no seats or backs, and the one bedroom littered with bed components, but no screws to assemble them. It was obviously at the bottom of the P.W.D's list.

Peter decided it would be simpler to remain at Kari during the week: the road was appalling and he spent most of his spare time trying to make sure the car (less than a year old) did not fall to pieces. We'd had five new tyres (re-treads unavailable), rear main-leaf springs, battery, engine mountings and shock absorbers replaced. An even bigger cost was insurance: mammy-wagon drivers were such a menace that premiums for all road users were astronomical.

It was the time of year when peasant farmers deliberately set fire to the land in order to get a fresh 'bite' of re-growth for their cattle. Of course, this destroys great tracts of precious woodland and the denuded countryside is soon useless, but when this happens, they just move on.

Peter had just returned from his morning's work and we were about to settle for the afternoon siesta when I became aware of a crackling sound outside. Looking out, I was petrified to see that we were completely surrounded by leaping flames, burning debris and glowing embers floating everywhere carried by strong wind from the desert, the harmattan.(See page 35.) In panic, I began running out to the car with everything I could pick up and it took all Peter's patience to reassure me that the fire-break he'd cleared around our vulnerable camp would protect us. He was right, although I couldn't help feeling we were extremely lucky that none of the smouldering embers flying about had been blown on to our highly combustible rumfa which would have gone up in smoke within seconds.

Perhaps I owed my nervousness to my 'delicate state' being half-way through pregnancy. My enlarging tummy presented problems: I had no means of buying maternity clothes and had to manage by borrowing Peter's shirts which I wore over the top of unzipped trousers.

Where to have the baby posed a problem, too. Doctors locally advised against first babies being born out here, as there were no means to cope if things went wrong. Also it would be foolish to take a new-born infant to the remote areas where Peter worked, often hundreds of miles from the nearest doctor or hospital. I badly wanted to return to my parents in the UK, but Peter had not seen his own parents for several years and had promised to do so during his end-of-tour leave. His father lived in Kenya and mother in Southern Rhodesia (as it was then). She had no permanent home anywhere, but suggested I should come to Bulawayo and stay in a small hotel where she had a room, and assured us that medical facilities were excellent.

So it was arranged that I should fly from Kano in mid-January before my 'airworthiness' expired, and Peter should join me and the baby, all being well, in early May. He would want to spend at least a month in Bulawayo with his mother, then we'd fly from Kenya to stay on the farm with his father for a further month, before returning to Nigeria.

Now I had somehow to find an urgent solution for the clothes problem. Peter had a couple of smart pyjama tops which I commandeered and adapted, but I could think of nothing remotely glamorous until I hit on the idea of utilising a pretty 'A-line' dress that I'd brought from the UK and had had very little opportunity to wear. I took it to pieces, discarding the long slim bodice and altered the skirt to turn it into a rather daring smock, with the erstwhile hip cuff becoming an off-the-shoulder neckline. Any dressmaker would have been horrified, but considering my complete lack of expertise, it was a surprising success.

Peter meanwhile was having to recruit labour for the scheme, of which he had sole charge and which extended over three provinces. He had to find four hundred men, then organise the building of camps to house them and their supervisors, 'mallams' whom he had already partly trained. They had to construct a network of roads, also clear thickets along the hundreds of streams (now mostly dry) where the bulk of the spraying was to take place.

His most important and most trying task was training the poorly-educated but over-confident mallams; so few of them were reliable that he was forever having to check up on the labourers' work himself, chivvying the mallams constantly, while organising stores, vehicles and equipment. At the same time he was continuing to survey and monitor the 'fly situation'.

In the rumfa we had several encounters with scorpions. Peter detected a slight movement under the edge of the tarpaulin covering the ground at the only doorway. Lifting it gingerly with a stick, he discovered a monstrous black one, which any of us might easily have stepped on, with extremely unpleasant consequences. Mohammedu invariably had bare feet, so he was even more at risk than us. Just a few hours later in the lamplight, I saw something on the floor and bent down to pick it up. In the nick of time I saw it was a scorpion, this time a smaller, red-brown one – deadlier than the big ones. Following Peter's earlier example, I dealt it a crushing blow with a bottle.

Christmas was not, after all, the non-event we'd feared, having expected to remain at Ririwai in isolation until my departure. Friends in Kaduna insisted we stay with them for a few days and we enjoyed the luxury of civilised living and happy festivities. I was able to take the opportunity to do some frantic shopping – my last chance.

But all too soon it was 'back to bush'. Peter hoped the arrival of a new Tsetse Officer would lessen his burdens, but Desmond, straight out from the UK, was more hindrance than help. Completely green, he lacked the sense to follow the advice Peter sent him before arrival – that he should come well-equipped and be sure to bring supplies with him. Instead, he came dressed entirely unsuitably and asked where the shops were.

There was news from HQ too, that another entomologist was to join the team. This should have encouraged Peter, but preliminary discussions had not gone well; he did not like the new man's attitude and feared that the project, into which he had put so much time and effort, might be jeopardised.

Unfortunately, all I could do was sympathise. It was almost time for difficult goodbyes. I was to go alone to a strange country, to stay with a woman I had never met, not in a home but an hotel, to have my first baby far from everyone I knew and loved, and there was no 'home' for me to return to.

Perhaps the fact that I had endured almost seven months of non-stop sickness prevented me from panicking. Perversely, as the plane took off from Kano early on January 17th, my spirits lifted with it, despite the pain of leaving Peter. And amazingly, at that instant, the nausea left me.

CHAPTER 9

First flight .... Heavenly, soaring high over the cloud-piles of fluffy meringues, soft and tempting, the world below mapped out in sunlight and shadow: empty plains, forested mountains, curvetting rivers and tiny, tiny dots that are all one can see of habitation.

After a sweltering, three hour delay at Leopoldville, made more frustrating because I could see nothing of our surroundings despite being close to the Congo River, the plane finally took off for South Africa where old friends met me at Johannesburg airport and whisked me off to their house in Natal to be spoiled for ten days. The contrast with Northern Nigeria was amazing. Here was a picture-book landscape, freshly green, of mountains and hills, valleys and streams. Long spells of warm sunshine were occasionally broken by the storms and showers of a South African summer, and there was a particular delight for me in the freedom from mosquito nets.

Arriving in Bulawayo at the beginning of February, I was greeted by an elegantly dressed lady in her fifties who introduced herself as Alice, Peter's mother. Accompanying her was Helen, friend and confidante, plump, comfortable and welcoming, who insisted I spend a couple of days at her home before moving to the hotel with mother-in-law.

Helen drove us to the smart suburb of Kumalo with its wide, immaculate avenues of palms and flowering trees, providing striking contrast to the brilliant white of the beautiful houses, half-hidden in the shrubberies of their lush gardens. Helen's house was among these, to me a palace of luxury after the privations of the past year, but equal to the material comforts indoors and the joy of the lovely garden complete with inviting swimming pool, was the warmth of friendship extended to me.

The Manor where I was to spend the next two months awaiting the arrival of the 'Little Treasure', was a modest residential hotel conveniently close to the main shopping centre where Alice worked in an exclusive boutique. Having lived alone for more than ten years since her divorce, she was delighted to have 'family' with her and had enthusiastically sewn and knitted endless baby clothes – a great relief for me, as I had expected to start from scratch. Shopping in Bulawayo was very pleasurable after Northern Nigeria: it was such a change not to have every request met with, 'It is finished' or 'One is all we have', and the town itself was delightful with its handsome buildings and quiet atmosphere.

There were, however, one or two clouds looming on the horizon ... How would I cope in a small hotel room with a newly-born baby? How could I let Peter know when the baby arrived. Contact was extremely difficult as he was so far from 'civilisation', where he would have to remain until the end of his tour at the beginning of May: mail could only be collected and sent when a vehicle from the scheme needed to go to Kaduna 140 miles away – perhaps once a week or ten days.

I was concerned that the letters he managed to get off indicated very low spirits. His fears for the scheme were materialising; his own position at the helm compromised by the entomologist's arrival. His growing anxiety about the hopelessness of the 'greenhorn', combined with his worries about me and the baby, made him very depressed.

As the weeks crawled by, I realised that The Manor was hardly a cheerful place for a month's leave when Peter finally got away, with or without a small baby. Most of the guests were elderly and I had plenty of time to study them .... There were Colonel and Mrs Lushington, ex-India colonials, he with a walrus moustache and stiff military bearing, endlessly re-living past campaigns, while she, large-bosomed and bottomed, downed a succession of glasses of sherry, her disapproving eye becoming slightly glazed and her gait unsteady by the time they adjourned to the dining room.

The armchair in the corner of the hotel lounge was invariably occupied by another ex-military man, Major Harrington, quite a jolly sort but rather garrulous. If he could find someone to listen, he liked to expound on the foibles of fellow man and put the world to rights. An occasional visitor was Stanley (I never learned his surname), who came to join his somewhat mannish lady-friend, Elsie, for a meal at weekends. Other guests appeared to shrink at his approach. Fifty-ish, balding, brisk and bristling, he would stride up and down rattling coins or keys in his pocket, conscious – or hopeful – that every eye was on him and his importance was noted. Somehow he demanded attention. The corner groups of conversationalists closed their ranks quickly and (they hoped) unobtrusively, so he would buttonhole a lonely victim whom he badgered with aggressive questions, answering himself loudly, with frequent sidelong glances round the room to see the effect of his remarks. The tension remained until Elsie appeared.

A soft-spoken, silver-haired gentleman of complacent rosiness who engaged various single ladies at the hotel in earnest conversations had attached himself to Alice for a time, but my arrival seemed to put him off, to my chagrin, though apparently not to hers. He transferred his interest to a glamorous, vital widow of unguessable age, and they took themselves off to night clubs or theatres: occasionally they sought privacy in the hotel garden and, being disturbed late one night by low voices from under my window, I peeped from behind the curtain. All I could see were two red spots – glowing cigarettes – under the black outline of a tree, then I recognised the voices and went hurriedly back to bed.

Baby Nicola eventually made her entrance at 11.30 p.m. on March 27th. My labour pains had begun fifteen hours earlier at The Manor, and after six hours I was taken to The Lady Rodwell Nursing Home, where the staff were kindness itself. I could not have had better care.

The next day I was amazed that flowers arrived from people I scarcely knew: some had even knitted baby clothes or made soft toys. My lovely Dr Ferguson even brought his wife in to see me, as he realised that Alice would probably be my only visitor, and they brought a cuddly pink rabbit for my baby.

It would have been a joyful occasion in other circumstances, but it was difficult, despite the great kindness shown to me, not to feel very alone. I had arranged with Alice to send Peter a cable immediately after the birth, but there was no response. Nothing.

To my relief, Helen suggested I bring baby Nicola to stay at her home until Peter arrived, or until Alice could find some accommodation to rent. Her kindness was particularly comforting as it was more than two weeks before I heard from Peter. His joy, I learnt later, was mingled with fury at the carelessness which had caused the delay. He had actually been in Kaduna HQ from the 28th to the 30th March; my cable had arrived on the 28th, but was not given to him. He returned to bush, and endured a further ten days of anxiety while the cable sat on a clerk's desk at HQ, until someone suggested it might as well go out with the next delivery of stores and mail to the scheme.

Eventually a batch of letters arrived for me from West Africa and amongst the expressions of happiness and longing to be with his new 'family' there were some very un-joyful things to report.

❧❧❧❧

Scorpions had become a serious menace at Kari, and despite constant vigilance, Peter did not escape. He was lying under the car doing the usual maintenance when an excruciating pain shot into his thigh. A small brown scorpion had climbed up his trouser leg, and Peter's agonised cries brought Mohammedu running. After dealing with the perpetrator, the steward managed to suck some of the poison out, then tried the traditional method of reducing the pain by breaking off the scorpion's tail and rubbing the liquid from it into the wound. While this didn't relieve the appalling burning agony of a thousand red hot needles thrust into his leg, the fact that Mohammedu had managed to remove some of the poison undoubtedly saved him from even worse effects. As it was, he endured more than 24 hours of torture, unable to sit, lie down, walk or stand with the slightest relief.

His weekend in Kaduna, which coincided, unknowingly, with Nicola's birth, also had some drama. He stayed with friends and in the middle of the night was woken by a loud bang, followed a few minutes later by the sound of tinkling glass. Peter climbed quietly out of the camp bed where he was sleeping in the lounge and tiptoed towards the kitchen. Gently pushing open the door, he saw a black shape poised on the sink, a 'teef-man', about to jump down. Peter bellowed at him at the top of his voice, and the man hastily turned and scrambled back out of the broken window. He hared off, pursued by Peter's shouts which he imagined would bring his host running, but they remained soundly asleep until he banged on their bedroom door .... Funnily enough it was the first time they'd ever had anyone staying in the house.

Back on the scheme problems with colleagues had obviously caused 'an atmosphere' to develop, not helped when they completely forgot to pay the labour force one week.

Yet more difficulties arose when a violent storm – unexpectedly early – left the 'office' in a foot of water. I suspected Peter of quietly crowing when he related how Desmond had attempted to cross a flooded ford at speed, and it had taken nearly twenty labourers to rescue him and push his vehicle out, in waist-high water. Travel was virtually impossible for several days, with the Kano river in yellow spate, bridges washed away and roads impassable. Peter and the steward had hastily hauled a tarpaulin over the rumfa but it rapidly sagged with the weight of water, and with the whole structure threatening to collapse, he had to climb up on to the roof in the torrential rain and 'bail-out' with a saucepan.

A somewhat alarming experience occurred when he was packing up the Ririwai camp. He looked up to see a troop of baboons approaching, the half-grown males leading the advance, grunting and making aggressive gestures, with short rushes towards him, sweeping the leaves off the rocks beside the track. Peter stood his ground and they eyed each other uncertainly for several minutes before the troop retreated noisily back the way they had come.

Reading the half-dozen letters, written over a ten-day period but arriving together, I saw that Peter was under considerable stress. Normally self-contained and good-natured, passionate about his work in attempting to eliminate one of the main scourges of Africa, sleeping sickness, he rose to the challenge of an early deadline for the successful completion of the scheme, which was a pilot project upon which depended international support for a major onslaught against the tsetse fly in West Africa. His single-mindedness made him out of sympathy with his colleagues, who, he considered, were unaware of the urgency demanded, and of what was ultimately at stake. He did admit that the 'rush tactics' they were all under pressure to use did not suit the two scientists who were accustomed to a slower, more methodical approach, but the frustrations of his situation and his current personal anxieties made him perhaps less tolerant than he might otherwise have been.

A climate of anxiety among Europeans was developing at this time, too, in Southern Rhodesia. Stunned by the news of Dr Verwoerd's assassination in South Africa, the general feeling was that the country should secede from the Federation (with Northern Rhodesia and Nyasaland) rather than 'hand over' to an African government. There were numerous cynical stories abounding about the failure of Sir Roy Welensky's attempts at positive 'Africanisation', though I personally felt that, in my short experience of the country, the races were too far apart in their daily lives to have any real understanding of each other. It was an interesting comparison with Nigeria, where colonial settlement had never been permitted and the British administration had, despite its faults, brought peace and stability, largely without inter-racial animosity.

Here among the white Rhodesians of British extraction, there was genuine but understandable fear for their future, especially if they were farmers, but also a realisation that change was inevitable and some, certainly, were prepared to compromise. The attitude of Afrikaner settlers was very different, however. Those that I came into contact with were much more belligerent and lacking in sensitivity. I often found myself wincing at their views, especially as this was soon after the massacre of innocent black South Africans at Sharpeville by Nationalist police.

How ironic that our own personal lives were about to be turned upside down by that faraway tragedy.

❧❧❧❧

It was May 1st when Peter finally arrived, and Baby Nicola was nearly six weeks old. By now, Alice and I were ensconced in a small rented house in a Bulawayo suburb and I was itching to surprise Peter with the news that we could have a car very cheaply indeed from an acquaintance of his mother.

It was going to be so exciting to explore this beautiful part of Africa, and I was especially looking forward to a couple of months in Kenya where I would meet my father-in-law and his wife, and Peter could show me the land he knew and loved so well.

The excitement and relief of reunion was brought to an abrupt end as soon as we were back in Heathfield Crescent and Alice took the baby out for a walk.

'I've been kicked out,' said Peter.

Unable to believe my ears, shell-shocked and trembling, I sank down on the sofa with Peter beside me, holding me close.

Gradually I made sense of what had happened, if 'sense' it could be called. Dr Wilson had been anxious for Peter to be engaged on a medium-term contract, but following 'Nigerianisation' these were only available to indigenous officers, so the Director was negotiating to get him signed up for a minimum of three tours. He was discussing the matter with an extremely officious Nigerian bureaucrat (whose political ambitions had recently received a setback when he lost an election), when the man caught sight of Peter's birthplace on the form – Johannesburg. He flew into an uncontrollable rage and virtually threw Dr Wiseman out of the office, refusing to listen to reason. 'How dare you ask for this man to be employed here!' he shouted. 'He is a murderer of African people!'

It was all utterly bewildering, until we made the connection with the report of the Sharpeville shootings only a few days before the fateful meeting. The man had ignored the fact that Peter had not set foot in South Africa since childhood and almost the whole of his adult life had been devoted to helping the African. Now he had been forced to quit Nigeria summarily, without even being given the chance to sort out his affairs. So here we were in a strange country, with no income, no job prospects, knowing nobody except Alice's friends, and with a new baby.

We spent our first week in May trying to make light of our predicament, doing a little sightseeing, making tentative enquiries about emigration to Australia and at the same time desperately attempting to enlist advice and/or help from the British High Commission in Salisbury (now Harare) – to no avail.

All the time we held on to the hope that post would arrive from Nigeria, perhaps apologising for the dreadful mistake ... The letter finally came, but brought no encouragement whatsoever. The news, in fact, was worse. The recompense for his outstanding and unstinting efforts was as follows:-

a) no contract; b) no leave salary; c) his car (which had necessarily been left there) would *not* be accepted in lieu of the balance due on it; d) our fares back to the UK would *not* be paid.

This was devastating, and Peter especially was plunged into depression. We had messages of sympathy from friends and colleagues, horrified at this treatment, but communication with Nigeria's officialdom was well-nigh impossible. All our worldly goods were there of course, and we had no hope of retrieving them.

Utterly disillusioned, Peter declared that he was finished with tsetse work and since we had drawn a blank with emigration possibilities, as well with our attempts to get a change of heart in Nigeria, we'd better head back to England. Whether we'd ever get our fares refunded was obviously unlikely, but we had no wish to stay in Africa. I was particularly thankful to be heading back to where, for me, was *home.*

CHAPTER 10

Once the decision had been made, we hastily sold the car (having had it for only a month), and the pram, paid the bills, mailed yet more letters of protest, and boarded a packed local plane, our precious infant precariously balanced on her over-loaded carry-cot.

At Salisbury, we changed planes and flew to Ndola in Northern Rhodesia, where we sweltered in the crowded airport until the Nairobi flight was called, by which time I had a dripping baby and a wet dress.

Still inexperienced enough to find flying exciting, I was glued to the window for glimpses of the mountains, serpentine rivers, vast lakes and strange ribbed hills below, when suddenly we were confronted with a most awesome sight: a giant volcano, the Donya Lengai, a perfect cone which rose, proud and sinister, iron-sided, so close that as the plane swept around its rim and banked to enable us to look down into its heart, it felt as if we would be sucked into its maw - a heart-stopping experience from which we had barely recovered when above a bank of cloud, rose the peak of Mount Kilimanjaro, impossibly magnificent.

Suddenly we were down to earth again, in Nairobi.

I'd often teased Peter that I'd only married him on the strength of his promise that we would live in Kenya, and he had been looking forward to having the chance, at last, of showing off the country he loved. But now, in our dramatically changed circumstances, there was barely time to be taken up to his father's home on Mount Eburu, walk round the farm with its very English herd of Red Devon cattle and a trout stream winding across it, before we were back in the Landrover and heading for the airport again.

The reunion with my parents was a mixture of joy and apprehension. We had no option but to inflict ourselves on their hospitality for Heaven knew how long. The house was small, but we had no other base from which to carry out our three-pronged campaign of protest, job-hunting and appeals to political figures in the UK and in Nigeria.

The following three months were occupied with all three and I was desperately hoping that Peter would find work in England, so that we could forget about West Africa, which at that time seemed like a bad dream.

Towards the end of September, it seemed my prayers were answered. Peter was offered a farm manager's job in Cambridgeshire on the strength of his diploma from the Royal Agricultural College. My elation died at birth. By the same post, a letter arrived from a senior colleague in Nigeria. He had had to take a number of documents to the Prime Minister's office for signature, and had included a contract for Peter. It was signed without a quibble and now the Department was awaiting his immediate return.

Within a week we were on a flight to Kano.

Our arrival at the airport produced a sharp reminder of what to expect in Nigeria at that time. The clerk at the Ministry had forgotten to book our onward flight to Kaduna, so we had to endure a six-hour journey by train for the last two hundred miles.

To our dismay, no accommodation had been arranged, either, and we were told we had better stay in the Catering Rest House for at least a month – not a pleasant prospect, especially with a small baby.

Fortunately Peter heard that a house at Mando Road, about five miles out, was empty, so after a few days we were able to move in. It was small but well-designed and thankfully, in good order, with french windows leading from the lounge on to a flower-filled patio. The wide eaves gave plenty of shade, so little Nicola could spend most of the morning out there, whenever there was a lull in the rains.

To our surprise, our old cook, Maman, was awaiting our return and greeted us enthusiastically. 'Oh Madam! I too glad to see you back! Much, much too glad!'

After such a rapturous welcome, we could hardly refuse him his former job, so, despite our reservations, back he came into the household, bringing with him a new 'small boy' who created far more work than he accomplished.

I was surprised to hear cheerful singing from just outside the window one morning, and looked out to see a troop of prisoners from the nearby jail file into our compound and begin to cut grass with pangas to the accompaniment of rhythmic chanting. This continued daily for the whole week, though not much was done as there were frequent rest periods and much laughter and fooling around. On the second morning I spotted our new 'small boy' slipping outside to hand round cigarettes. This put me in a quandary. They were almost certainly Peter's cigarettes, but they may have been a form of 'protection money': certainly the supervision of the convicts was almost non-existent. I was glad there were no doors on that side of the house.

Three weeks after moving in, the Ministry decided we must move out – within twelve hours! We were packing furiously (in every sense) when a message arrived to say the move should be delayed for 48 hours. Hardly had that sunk in and we'd begun to work out how we could live out of packed boxes and cases for two days, when another instruction was delivered, telling us that the move should be delayed for a further 24 hours ... and this just days before our departure for 'bush'.

We were in the 'new' house for six days, long enough to have to put up the curtains, then take them down again and pack up baby, belongings and all, before heading out of Kaduna

Peter's project required that, as before, we would have to have a base in Gombe, a prospect I did not relish in the least. My worst fears were realised when we opened the door of our new 'home'. It was indescribably filthy, and after the briefest inspection, we retreated rapidly to the local Rest House where we'd have to cope with Baby Nicola for at least a week, while the place was cleaned up.

Fortunately Peter was able to spare two labourers from his scheme, and they, with our 'house-boys' prepared to attack floors, walls and furniture with buckets of soapy water, scrubbing brushes, plus – a horrid sight – all my brand new dusters, together with scourers and gallons of disinfectant.

Gathering my wits after the initial shock of seeing this 'Black Hole', I inspected the mattresses *...ugh!* The previous occupants had plainly never used bed linen; neither had they bothered to get out of bed for what one assumes is sometimes necessary during the night.

Peter went immediately to the Yard Superintendent but met with a belligerently defensive attitude. Yes, he did know what an appalling state the house had been left in: he'd informed the District Officer who had declined to inspect it, so he'd decided to do nothing himself .... No, he did not intend to do anything about it now either. It was with the greatest difficulty that Peter managed to extract a promise that the mattresses would be replaced.

When the 'new' ones arrives, however, they were in as bad a state as the originals, which we refused to have in the house. The man who brought them spun a yarn about 'only transport dirt', so I jumped into the car and drove straight to the Yard Superintendent's office. He neither got up from his chair, nor looked up from the newspaper he was reading when I arrived. I insisted that he confirm the driver's story that the mattresses were brand-new, or else explain where they came from, but was met with stony silence. Eventually he shrugged and said we'd be better off with the first ones! I was absolutely stunned. 'And what about mosquito nets?' I demanded. So full of enormous holes they were quite beyond repair. He replied sarcastically that he would have them *washed* at the Rest House at his own personal expense.

Feeling so angry, it was difficult to speak, I told him I'd never seen such a filthy place in my life. He suggested that I didn't know Gombe was a bush station ....! In a most unpleasant tone he invited me to 'have the privilege' of inspecting his store, but I got no change there: the two men in charge of it were insolent and utterly unhelpful.

In despair we went to the D.O's office where the 'nice John Mayhew' we'd heard about in Kaduna flapped his arms helplessly and told us with a weak grin, 'This is Nigeria 1960, and it is to be expected...'

❧❧❧❧

The day following our skirmishes with the Yard Superintendent and the D.O. we went to tea with the only old friends still around since the previous year. There we learned that Mayhew was the most unpopular man on the station, a snooper and a meddler whose favourite pronouncement was, 'Of course, back in the 1890s...'

Though we had been determined to 'take as we found', Peter returned from the D.O's office – to which he had been peremptorily summoned – literally hopping with rage. He had been aggressively grilled for more than an hour, with Mayhew rudely insinuating that neither he nor the Tsetse Unit were either qualified for or capable of the task they had come expressly to carry out. He attempted to impose his own completely ignorant ideas on the whole scheme, to Peter's great embarrassment and indignation. In a final twist he insisted we return later for midday drinks despite Peter's polite refusal in view of the fact that we were in the throes of trying to move into our hateful house.

Extremely annoyed, we did however turn up at 1 p.m., to find no host, two naked children and a very harassed wife who plainly found it beyond her powers to entertain anyone. Baffled by the situation, we twiddled our thumbs for an hour until Mayhew finally appeared – with another guest in tow. He made no apologies and addressed what little conversation he was capable of entirely to the man he had brought with him.

We left even more crossly than we had arrived.

Back at the house, we put up our camp beds in the 'mosquito room' where at least we could get whatever breeze there was in the night, and I began lengthening curtains. Fortunately I'd made them all eight feet long, and simply had enormous hems where the windows were small. In all, they were adapted for at least twenty houses in Nigeria alone.

Baby Nicola had no cot, so we put pillows and blankets round her camp bed in case she fell out and I sewed up twenty-four large holes in one of the existing nets in the house. The other was past redemption, but fortunately we had nets for the camp beds. So despite gaping cracks in the walls alongside exposed wiring and unfinished points for the long-awaited advent of *electricity*, we made the house into some sort of home.

A painfully chewed finger told me that Nicola had cut her first tooth and we were as full of jubilation as if we'd done the whole thing ourselves. By now she was mobile in every direction, except straight ahead, and loved to 'stand on her head' – legs straight, bottom in the air, surveying her toes and the upside-down world between her legs, just like the flamingoes in *Alice*. She attracted much attention from passing Fulani women, bejewelled and bangled from head to toe. One of them slipped off one of her many bracelets and placed it gently on Nicola's plump little arm. They all wanted to caress her, run their fingers through her silver-blond hair, exclaiming, no doubt, over her pinkness and her blue eyes. Pleased as I was by their admiration, I was secretly terrified when they bent over her without ever removing the enormous calabashes they carried on their heads. I needn't have worried: their sense of balance was simply miraculous, and they moved with an elegance that models on the Paris catwalk could never match.

Within days, Baby Nicola was having her first experience of life on safari, and, judging by her gleeful antics in the playpen under a shady tree, thoroughly enjoying it. Now late October, we should have had some relief from 'the little hot season', but there was no sign of the harmattan and the thermometer frequently reached 100° before midday.

Just after settling her for her afternoon sleep and collecting her toys from the playpen, I heard a soft 'plop' and saw a greeny-yellow chameleon lying a couple of yards away. It seemed winded, didn't move for ages and when it did so, raised itself unbelievably slowly and unsteadily, sinking flat on to the ground again after a few seconds. Rising painfully again it took a few steps, each one as it if were its last, its mouth gaped wide and it keeled over on to its side. Peter gently picked it up and put it in the shade by the entrance to the rumfa, but an hour or so later, on his way out to catch grasshoppers to feed a hornbill that had adopted us since our arrival, he called me to witness the strangest sight: another, smaller chameleon, silvery grey-green, was climbing over the motionless body – now a corpse. It was plainly a male, and he tried vainly and pathetically to mate with the dead female. He found her stillness inexplicable and gazed at her from every angle, moved across her body again and again to try and elicit some response, some flicker, then bewildered, perhaps heartbroken, he moved – oh so slowly – away, lifting each leg as though he could not bear to put it down and remove himself further from her. After only three or four steps he paused, looked back and, as though buoyed by sudden hope, hastened back to her side. In vain.

We feared we had another tragedy on our doorstep the very next day when 'Monty' disappeared. He was a young hornbill that Peter had rescued from a labourer's hungry clutches. We christened him 'Montgomery' for his imperious attitude, beady eyes and over-large beak.

He was a hard taskmaster, clucking impatiently if we failed to produce his meals of juicy grasshoppers on time, and catching them was no easy matter. Sometimes I could persuade him to take a little sliced tomato if we'd failed miserably on our grasshopper hunt. Nicola was rather wary of him, understandably, since he had once mistaken her fingers for fat pink worms. I discovered how painful that was when he made the same error with my toes. But really he was a poppet, hopping on to our shoulders in a friendly fashion, nuzzling us with his beak, just to show there were no hard feelings, even though we were pretty rotten parents.

For two days we searched fruitlessly: no tiny chirrups, no perky little black-and-white figure hopping homeward. We despaired, knowing only too well what his fate would be ... On the afternoon of the third day, just as Peter got out of the car after his day's work on the scheme, a tiny, triumphant Montgomery appeared at the drive entrance, greeted us both warmly and settled down to a banquet of grasshoppers that Peter had brought back to the house 'just in case'.

A simultaneous crisis that had been building up for days was more difficult to deal with. Maman's aversion to work, especially when we had to go on tour, was making him 'very sick; much too sick'. At first he complained of pains in one leg, which apparently became so bad he could not sleep and cried all night, so he told us in a faint whisper. We were in a quandary. Peter went to talk to him in his gida (hut), where he was sufficiently far from death's door to cry vehemently 'I very sick, two both!'. So now it was the other leg as well. We asked Dr White to visit, but after a thorough examination the verdict was, 'He's shamming – you'll have to sack him'. But we could hardly fire someone who said they were too ill to rise; on the other hand, we had to have a reliable cook. Mohammedu, the steward, was coping marvellously, but there were frequent occasions when the services of both men were vital. It had been becoming more and more obvious that this 'bad, too bad sickness' always developed just as a safari trip was imminent. For a time we procrastinated, and Mohammedu coped.

A nasty incident involving Peter's mallams took our minds off Maman, temporarily. It was their pay-day and they should have arrived at Mallam Sidi at noon to receive their money. By one o'clock Peter was extremely worried and was about to institute a search when they arrived, panting and dishevelled, to report being attacked. They had been cutting 'fly-paths' near the village of Garin Yarima when children who were guarding the shambas from baboons took fright at the appearance of strangers and had run home screaming. Without seeking explanations, the village men and their headman launched an attack on the mallams with axes, clubs and bows and arrows. Fortunately no one was seriously hurt, though they were all shocked and frightened. Peter brought home some of the arrows; they were barbed, so injury could have been very nasty. Peter hurried over to the District Head who reacted speedily to his report and the attackers were arrested the same day.

Back at the house, we wondered briefly if our protests about its terrible state had had an effect, as one Monday morning two men arrived carrying tins of paint and announced they were going to paint the plaster around the new (unfinished) light fittings. One of them walked all round the house – slowly. An hour later the other one also walked slowly round. After much discussion they painted six small bricks outside the house, then disappeared.

The next day, both turned up again. 'Where's your ladder?' I asked. 'No ladder, madam,' they replied indicating a huge 44-gallon oil drum full of dirty water which they indicated they would stand on. 'Oh no!' I protested. 'Please use a ladder!'

An hour of thinking ensued ... they disappeared. Two hours later they were back, this time with an enormous contraption, the sort used in bridge-building. It was filthy, but they proposed bringing it inside. Patiently I pointed out that it was far too big even to get through the door .... More thinking .... End of Day Two.

Wednesday. This morning they arrived only with paint tins. They sat on the verandah and thought.... Two hours went by. Peter returned from work and lost his temper. 'Get a step ladder! *Now! For heaven's sake!*' They disappeared hastily. One hour later they were back again bearing in triumph a *giant* ladder (filthy, inevitably) which they plonked down flat on the carpet, grinning. After a few minutes the realisation finally dawned on them – the ladder was as least twice the height of the house. They picked it up, perilously and discontentedly, and took it outside. Bravely, I asked when they were going to paint the house properly. 'When we have painted these small-small,' a wave towards the dangling light 'fittings' – actually bare wires...

They left. We didn't see them again.

A few days later Peter drove to the Public Works officer in the slight hope that he might be able to persuade the Yard Superintendent to get things moving, but on pushing open the door, having received no response to his knock, he found the man slumped over his desk. Peter hurried over to him, thinking he must be ill, but two whisky bottles, both empty, at his feet, told the story. He lifted his head briefly. 'Go 'way. Go 'way,' he muttered. There was no point in staying.

Towards the end of November, we had an unexpected visit from Bill Kirkby, who had driven over from Kaduna. Weary after such a long and trying journey, he was relieved that we were able to offer him a meal, though we had no spare bed fit to sleep on, as we were still without mattresses. While Mohammedu and I made preparations (Maman had not risen from his Bed of Pain for nearly two weeks) a large Mercedes came into the drive, and we were summoned outside by peremptory hooting. Without greeting or preamble, the District Officer tried to insist that Bill leave us and come to his own house for dinner, and when we, as tactfully as we could, pointed out that arrangements were already in hand, he drove off without a word. Bill paid him a courtesy call in the morning, en route to the work in progress on the scheme, and discovered for himself that the man was as intransigent and insufferable as we had warned. Mayhew's attempt to browbeat the Principal Veterinary Officer of the Northern Region on matters concerning the tsetse eradication work and Fulani cattle-grazing, met with an icy response and a rapid end to the conversation.

Life on the home front was enlivened by the rapid transition of the Little Treasure to the Little Menace, who, at barely eight months, was into every kind of mischief. She discovered the joys of 'mountaineering', so, perched on the top of chairs or sofa, she could reach whatever we thought was safely out of reach. Tearing up paper, especially her father's laboriously typed reports, was a particular joy, and everything she picked up had to be experimentally swallowed. Vocal activity was equally important and she practised squealing and squeaking to express gleeful excitement on nabbing yet another trophy.

Outside, the volume she produced depended on the mode of transport: in her pushchair she serenaded us with seraphic sweetness: in the car she stood up triumphantly and bellowed at full blast till we were nearly deafened.

Monty was also making greater demands on our attention. Growing rapidly in size and appetite, he summoned us by making determined little sallies, with wings outstretched, at our fingers – or toes, if available. It was often impossible to find grasshoppers (for which I was secretly relieved – it always made me think of feeding Christians to the lions, as they had to be alive). We tried scraps of raw meat, tomatoes and pasta. It was surprising he didn't care for bananas, but he ate sardines and Rice Krispies for breakfast with relish.

Sadly he did not pester us for very much longer. One morning he failed to appear at the usual time and despite our searches, this time there was no happy ending – at least, not for us. We could only hope that, young and vulnerable as he was, he was learning to cope on his own in the wild.

It rapidly became obvious that we had to face up to a decision regarding Maman. Dr White had examined him on three occasions, but could find nothing wrong. Meanwhile, although admittedly 'recovered', he refused to stir from his gida, and Mohammedu, while managing wonderfully, could not possibly continue on his own when Peter was so frequently on tour.

Eventually Peter told Maman he would have to be sent back to Kaduna. We needn't have worried. He was delighted. The lassitude of the past few weeks miraculously disappeared and whatever sympathy we'd had evaporated completely when we discovered him trying to slip off with two new uniforms, lent for the period of employment with us.

The 'small boy' also wanted to return to Kaduna, so yet another one had to be found. Within hours, not entirely unexpectedly, an urchin turned up on the doorstep asking for a job, and though we were doubtful about references, we took Adamu on trial.

Christmas was looming, but Gombe's limitations, not to mention the time necessarily spent 'in bush', made traditional preparations impossible. No cards were available from the SIM shop despite assurances that they would arrive by November, but since we'd discovered that a telegram took nine days from Gombe to Kaduna, it was unrealistic to hope that any mail would reach our families at home by a certain time. We managed a quick trip to Jos in between tours at Mallam Sidi, and were thankful to find presents for each other and for the Treasure.

We were finally able to return to Gombe two days before Christmas, and apart from all the others things to do, there were six 'hair-dos' I'd promised to give, and I had to devise some means of decorating the house, and give a party for friends.

We found the small number of European Gombe residents unusually cheerful, mainly because of the news that the inebriated Yard Superintendent had been packed off: perhaps there was now hope that we might at last get some mattresses, plugs for the washbasin and sink, and even that the numbskulls who wanted to paint 'small-small' round the bare wires (still waiting for fittings, never mind power), might re-appear.

There were week-long celebrations, starting off with a Pyjama Party when those of us with only 'shorties' had to brave the wolf-whistles and ribald suggestions from some of the men. Unfortunately the Club House was almost a no-go area for the whole holiday, as the cotton ginnery men all went on a continuous booze there and the atmosphere was hardly welcoming to families. One of the drunks turned up at the Christmas dinner party of our friends and made himself so objectionable that the evening was ruined. He staggered into the bedrooms where guests had left their sleeping children and pulled them all out of bed – including Baby Nicola, who howled with indignation for the next hour. He refused to put Nicholas, our host's infant back in his cot, and Susan was reduced to angry tears of frustration.

During the meal, which should have been a very special occasion, Susan and David having gone to so much trouble, he sat opposite me, leering and making loud, vulgar comments. I had never felt so uncomfortable or so furious, to think that our hosts should have to stand for this. Somehow they remained politely calm, then to general relief he got up and disappeared. For five minutes we all relaxed and began to enjoy ourselves, believing that one of the men had managed to persuade him into the car and had taken him home.

Suddenly silence fell. We all froze, as Harry staggered back into the room and fell, face down on to the carpet.

Unfortunately he was not completely unconscious and fought violently against the efforts of several guests to remove him bodily. It was another twenty minutes before they subdued him sufficiently to carry him out and tip him into the back of a pick-up truck belonging to the Forestry Officer who, at last, was able to get rid of him.

Our own party was on Boxing Day, and I was hard put to it to create a festive look to the house. Eventually we found a small thorn tree and I decorated its bare branches with shiny balls, and a bit of tinsel and 'snow'. I also concocted pleated circles out of navy wrapping paper (off cotton wool rolls) and yellow typing paper which I hung up. Peter brought in some beautiful bombax flowers which looked wonderful by candlelight on the dining table. One advantage of the absence of electricity was that, in the evening, the ugliness of the house was effectively disguised by the soft light of the oil lamps and candles.

So, the end of 1960 was happier than we might have hoped for earlier in the year, despite the constant nausea of my second pregnancy, and the frequent bouts of dysentery that defied the usual treatments. Baby Nicola was thriving and Peter deeply involved in preparation for his main scheme (the pilot project having proved successful) to be centred around the Matyoro lakes. We prepared to move out to his new camp as soon as the holiday was over.

Mohammedu with Nicola

CHAPTER 11

Before getting a camp established on the Matyoro, Robert had some clearing up to do at Mallam Sidi, so we spent the first few days of January in the old rumfa which had become virtually a second home. I was uneasy about having to leave Adamu, the new 'small boy' in charge of the Gombe house while we were away: he seemed sullen and was unwilling to learn his tasks from Mohammedu.

My fears were realised. We returned to find the house ransacked and much that was irreplaceable had gone. Fortunately the main bedroom where Peter kept his clothes was locked, but I was not so lucky and lost not only dresses and the two sweaters brought from England, but lengths of material urgently needing to be made up for a 'lady-in-waiting'. The new slide projector bought in Jos only just before Christmas and Peter's camera had gone – and once again, the complete contents of the laundry basket with good bed-linen and towels. It was shattering.

The 'teef-man' appeared to have broken in through the bathroom window, but remembering our experience with Dalmia, Peter investigated where the broken glass had fallen. Sure enough it was all *outside* the house.

The police took Adamu into custody, and also arrested his brother, very well known to them, who, we discovered, had been living in our compound without our knowlege.

When we went back out to bush, we left a 'maigardi' in charge of its security. Mohammedu found a new 'small boy' from his own home area, Biu, which pleased us, as although 'Musa' was completely green, 'Biu boys' had a reputation for honesty and hard work.

From Mallam Sidi, Peter drove me along the newly-cut tracks for a preview of our new 'home' at the lakes. It was late afternoon and the sun had lost its fierceness. For once we saw abundant wildlife: several families of baboons, monkeys chasing through the trees, an eagle which perched on a branch just above the car when we passed, with a long thin snake in its beak. Just then a russet-brown bushbuck hurled itself out of a thicket beside the track and tore across in front of us – gone before we could blink.

Peter had designed a much more spacious and comfortable rumfa than the one we were leaving. Perfectly positioned only about fifty yards from the water's edge in the shade of an enormous tamarind tree, it boasted a covered 'verandah', as well as two bedrooms and a pantry. Entirely constructed from straw matting, the slightest breeze was able to penetrate the walls and we were to discover to our amazement and pleasure that, because of its proximity to the lake, night time temperatures dropped dramatically, sometimes by as much as 40°, and we would need bedtime blankets.

The Matyoro is a string of several lakes and our camp was beside the central, biggest one. Even though, by the time we'd moved in, Peter had had to fire the

Bathtime in the bush

undergrowth in the area prior to spraying operations, it was still a refreshing change of scene and, sitting on the verandah, we watched and listened for animal and bird life surrounding us – a perfect vantage point. Strangely-shaped tree skeletons rose from the water like grotesque statues, which, like their city counterparts, offered resting sites and 'a bird's eye view' not to pigeons, but to cormorants and herons enjoying this fishing paradise.

Within hours of moving in, I saw my first crocodile: noting a disturbance in the water on our side of the lake we went quietly close to the edge, scanning the surface, and there he was, his bulging eyes and the knobbly ridge of his snout so easy to mistake for a floating log. He returned our gaze for a minute or so, then slowly submerged among the water lilies. I was very nervous that we should be living so close to the lake's edge: I hadn't realised that there might be crocodiles but Peter was cheerfully confident there was no danger. 'They'll probably take themselves off to one of the other lakes now we're here,' he said. I was not so sure, but forgot my worries once I discovered the fascination of trying to identify the myriad tracks of game animals in the sandy paths around us. On the first day I saw the hoof-prints of the dainty little duiker, large and small paw marks, the former those of hyaena, the others of civet (a small member of the cat family) as well as the gay roundabout tracks of a flock of guinea fowl.

The peaceful calm of it all drew me out early each morning, and before the day's heat became too intense I walked alongside the water's edge, the sunlight gilding the surface as the water lilies shyly unfolded their petals of tenderest lilac-blue.

A brief return trip to Gombe was delayed en route by more than an hour by the antics of a large troop of baboons that we encountered in the forest. There were at least sixty individuals in three or four distinct groups, but it was the largest of these that took our attention.

We'd surprised a huge fellow who was snoozing in a tree beside the track and, seeing us, was so overcome with astonishment that he simply could not make up his mind what to do or where to go. We stopped, and the troop, reassured by the lack of movement, let their curiosity overcome their nervousness and they surrounded the car, surveying us from every conceivable angle, and looking disconcertingly human as they scratched their heads, or sat with elbows on their knees, chin in hand, until they decided that other matters were more pressing, and left.

Although amusing to watch, their vicious yellow fangs are an indication that no liberties should be taken. Peter warned me that, should I meet a troop on my own, I must beat a careful retreat. Males are particularly aggressive and I had a fright the following week when, during my morning stroll with Nicola we almost walked into the middle of a group. Alerted by a warning bark, I turned and headed quickly back for the rumfa, scarcely daring to look behind me until the fierce sounds faded, holding Nicola so tightly she could hardly breathe, seized as I was by a sudden fear that she might be snatched away.

Hyaena spoor around the lake also caused spasms of panic. Peter had told me that they had been known to slink into tents at night and attack sleepers. I had heard distant howling during the day, but they did not come near the camp until one night we were woken sometime after midnight by a loud yowl that seemed to come from just the other side of our flimsy wall of straw. Peter immediately leapt out of bed, grabbed the torch and dashed outside leaving me trembling and anxious in the dark until he returned some ten minutes later saying he'd frightened it away. 'They're utter cowards,' he assured me when he saw how terrified I was.

Sometimes my husband's courage seemed to verge on bravado, though I didn't feel qualified to remonstrate. Being one of those people 'who in a perilous emergency thinks with her legs', I was frozen with fear the afternoon he decided to 'sail' on the lake on our inflatable lilo, with the baby's cot sheet as a sail. He spent a happy hour tacking to and fro, while I sat holding Nicola, almost paralysed with anxiety, imagining that he was being followed by the quietly sinister, imperceptible ripple of a crocodile closing in .... as usual, my fears were laughed at.

Boating on the Matyoro

Returning to Gombe again to collect stores and mail, we were bemused by a letter from the Doma Native Court, where Adamu and his brother had been tried for the theft of our property. Scarcely had we finished reading it when Adamu himself strolled, unannounced and grinning into the lounge.

'What on earth are you doing here?' demanded Peter.

'Sah, I swear on Bible I no steal, so they let me go. I come for my money, sah.'

Checking again with the Sergeant, we learned that, at the outset, both had freely admitted their guilt, but changed their story later, so had been allowed to go free.

We read ....

Doma Native Court
Gombe, 30th January, 61.

Mr. P.J. Aitchison,
Tsetse & Tryps Unit,
Veterinary Division,
Gombe.

Adamu Kilba's and Tata's Case.

I have to inform you that one Ben charged the above named two persons for stealing on 5/1/61. The Police were made to investigate and report to me. Ben was even made to swear on 17/1/61 that the two persons did steal. The police did their best to find out the truth of the case and to find out whether they could get the stolen pooperty, but up to date 30/1/61 they could not get that.
For that reason, the court made Adamu Kilba and Tata swear that they did not steal and they do not know the person who stole the property. They were acquitted.
But still the police are invetigating, and if they or you have any information concerning the case, you could report, and the case be heard afresh.

Another item in the post was a letter from mother-in-law, telling us of her intention to visit us shortly. This was alarming, given our present circumstances, plus the fact that I was suffering from 24-hour-a-day pregnancy sickness. Peter wrote post-haste, saying we'd be delighted to see her, but *not* in Gombe and *not* in the hot season which would still be in full swing until about the end of June.

Preparations for the promised electricity also caused problems. One morning I found two men in the lounge removing pictures from the wall and knocking in four large holes. In response to my surprised enquiry, they said they were installing the meter. Surely it didn't have to go in the middle of the sitting room wall? Oh yes, I was told. All the houses on the station were having meters put in the same place. Incredulous, we leapt into the car and did a quick tour: sure enough, *none* of the others had the meter in the lounge; they were all either in the garage or in some totally inconspicuous place. After a long argument, the man in charge backed down and the meter was moved to the garage.

The very next day more workmen arrived, this time armed with saws as they prepared to remove one of the few precious trees in the garden and put up a pole right outside the front door. Again we felt we must protest, as much for the sake of future occupants as for ourselves, so the C.C.S. was fetched once more and to our surprise and relief, agreed that it could quite well be moved to a more convenient spot.

Back at the lakes, I received a surprise visit from the District Head who had been invited to inspect the scheme's progress. He called at the rumfa, together with his scribe and lesser officials, to offer his greetings. A wizened, slight figure, he nevertheless possessed great dignity and charm, and although initially our mutual ignorance of the other's language made for some awkwardness, this dissolved immediately I introduced Baby Nicola. She was the centre of attention and admiration for the whole visit and they would have all held her in turn had she not been overwhelmed by the many strange faces and clung to me, close to tears.

Nigerians have an instinctive love of children, frequently strangers approached us with arms outstretched and begged to pick her up.

Crowding around to see the white baby

Two nights later there was a near-tragedy at the labour camp about four miles from ours, when the rumfa belonging to Umaru, Peter's right-hand-man, went up in flames and was destroyed within two minutes. The youngest child had just been put to bed when his mosquito net caught fire and the rumfa was engulfed in seconds. Umaru rushed in and pulled him from the blazing bed, his own clothes set alight as he did so. Quickly the whole compound was ablaze, his two wives and the other Mallams managing to salvage a few possessions, but half of all he owned was lost, including his store of food and his fowls. The baby escaped, miraculously, with superficial burns.

During March the harmattan arrived, bringing relief from daily temperatures of around 105° in the shade. While this made living more comfortable, it was counter-productive as regards the scheme, since hot weather was needed to drive the tsetse flies down on to the tree trunks and the under-side of lower branches, where the carefully sprayed insecticide was waiting for them. Although most of the huge tsetse population had now been eliminated, it was essential that the scheme produced 100% success.

At the end of May, when the heat was back at its most blindingly oppressive, we were instructed to move to Kaduna. So, coping with Nicola, suddenly a very active toddler, and a distressed and fretful Alice who had insisted on coming to stay at the very time and place we had strongly warned she should avoid, and still being wretchedly sick myself, somehow the packing had to be done.

On a scorching day in early June we set out optimistically on the two-day journey. Unfortunately luck did not go with us, and within fifty miles the car came to a juddering halt. Peter was furious when he saw what had happened: the 'new' fanbelt put in by the Gombe mechanic was in fact old and worn, and had broken. Somehow he managed a temporary repair and we limped unhappily on to Bauchi. There, the local mechanic was about to have his siesta. and it took some angry words even to get him, sullenly, to give the necessary parts for Peter to do the job himself. Without the appropriate tools it took a long time, and with several hours of bad road ahead, it was quite difficult to hide anxiety from an already distraught Alice. Somehow we made it, and the Jos garage took the car in next morning. By eleven we were on our way again, and arrived safely in Kaduna in the early evening.

We had only to endure two days in the unwelcoming Rest House before we were able to move into a little house which had just two beds. Peter went to the P.W.D. store to ask for another, since there was nowhere for Alice to sleep, and we were amazed when a truck drew up a few hours later and unloaded a bedstead. However, that was it. No mattress. Another trip to the store was not so successful; for some reason it didn't seem possible to produce a mattress as well as a bedstead. Peter gave up and we borrowed one from the Wilsons.

Within days of our arrival Nicola was very poorly: crying with tummy-ache, her knees drawn up under her, she breathed in gasps and her little body was stiff with tension. Given an anti-malarial drug by the doctor, she couldn't keep it down, so we were directed to the Nursing Home where she would have in-treatment. This was not the dependable sanctum I had fondly imagined when I booked in for the coming birth of No. 2. The disorganisation and carelessness of most of the staff was alarming and would undoubtedly have prolonged Nicola's illness if I hadn't stayed in with her and personally given her medicine at the prescribed times. It was a relief to take her home.

Unfortunately I went down with a severe bout of malaria just a few days later, and after a horrendous night of vomiting, acute pain, and the sensation of a huge head, threatening to explode any second, I was packed off to hospital myself.

Still in my nightdress, I was made to stand, despite shivering uncontrollably and unable to remain on my feet without support, at the end of a long queue of people who appeared to be waiting for prescriptions. The Hausa nurse could not – or would not - understand that Dr Adler had already seen me and sent me for admittance (he was in charge of the hospital, but so overworked that it was impossible for him to supervise the nursing staff). After an interminable wait during which Peter practically went down on his knees for me to sit somewhere, I was taken to a ward and a bed pointed out – with complete indifference – and I was left to collapse on to it.

The big worry was that the unborn baby might have been affected, but there was no way of knowing.

After three days in hospital, I found myself transferred to a convalescent home run by Catholic nuns, mostly Irish. The jolly but formidable Sister looking after me insisted that an essential constituent of treatment should be a bottle of Guinness every day, and I found myself in trouble if I didn't drink every drop. Hating the stuff, I learned to hide it under the pillow and give it to Peter during visiting hours, and he made sure there was always an empty bottle waiting for Sister Assunta.

When I was finally allowed home I began counting the days to the E.T.A.

Mid-August came and went, to my dismay, as not only was I having the usual discomforts of end-of-pregnancy, but I was still being constantly sick. There were several false alarms, when labour appeared to start, then change its mind a couple of hours later, until the 24th when at midnight there was a great whoosh of blood and staggering pain. Somehow I got into the car and Peter raced to the Nursing Home where Joanna was safely delivered within minutes by Sister Owol, a smiling, reassuring Yoruba lady.

All seemed fine: Peter went home and Sister disappeared to write her report, leaving me in the care of two Hausa nurses with strict instructions that they must attend to my tummy.

The two girls stood facing each other on either side of me in the delivery room, not in a symbolic guardianship of their charge, but in a togetherness from which I was completely excluded. It was as though I was invisible, just a lumpy shape under the sheet. Laughing and chattering they were completely oblivious to anything beyond their own titbits of gossip and as I lay inert, a feeling of unease gradually spread over me. I could not explain it, but I found myself praying that the Sister would return quickly.

At last she did and took in the situation at a glance.

'What have you two been doing all this time?' she screamed. 'Why haven't you called me?'

Pushing one aside and sending the other off to fetch a hypodermic needle, she started massaging my tummy, which by now had become so swollen with blood that the pressure sent a crimson stream gushing out over the white sheets. The vigorous kneading was painful but when I mentioned it, rather faintly, she turned on me fiercely.

'It's better to hurt now than you lie dying!' she snapped. I was shocked into silence and watched listlessly as the flow refused to be staunched and the deep stain spread over fresh sheets, more fresh sheets, and yet more. The Hausa girl arrived with the needle.

'Can't you see this is broken? And it's dirty! I cannot use it!' Sister Owol's face contorted with contempt. She was so furious she could hardly find the words she wanted to throw at the Hausas.

Again she had to leave me and run to find a needle herself. As she stormed back into the delivery room her voice was almost a shriek.

'Don't you know there are *no facilities* for blood transfusions in this hospital? If this woman dies, her blood will be on *your* hands! Your neglect may have cost her her life!'

What a strange sensation it was to lie there knowing my existence on earth was slipping away with the unstoppable haemorrhage, that these might be my last hours ... How would Peter cope with Nicola? And the new baby, whom I'd hardly seen, just held her for a moment before she was taken away, wrapped up like a little papoose, all pinkly wrinkled and with a tuft of dark hair on the top of her head? I'd never know her...

Strangely, I felt quite calm. There was nothing I could do but wait. The balance was in God's hands, through Sister Owol. How would He tilt it? I prayed, though without any feelings of hope, while the Yoruba Sister's implacable hands refused to surrender, and for two long hours she kneaded my sponge-like womb without pausing.

2 a.m. ... 3 a.m. ... Then the miracle. The blood flow slowed and stopped. Sister Owol smiled and touched my hand, and I was wheeled to a ward.

Surprisingly I recovered quickly from the haemorrhage, despite having lost a great deal of blood. I seemed quite fit, apart from the everlasting dysentery which I could never seem to shake off.

I breast-fed Joanna and she was thriving. I thought that now I could begin to savour life, after nine months of sickness and the crisis at Joanna's birth.

It was the second week of November, when I had had violent diarrhoea all night and it continued through the morning. After giving Baby Joanna her 2 p.m. feed I put her in her cot and settled Nicola for her afternoon rest. As I walked back into the lounge, a strange crawling sensation began at the back of my neck and spread insidiously all over my body.

Something told me I needed help. Urgently I tried to reach the next-door house, but after staggering for barely a couple of yards, hit the gravel drive with a thump.

Someone must have seen me and taken me to the hospital, but I was aware of nothing, beyond a tightening, strangling vice that was contorting all my limbs into an agonising skewed posture.

As I swam in and out of consciousness, I was vaguely aware of a sea of faces above me and a wall of white coats all round the bed. As if from very far away, I heard a voice say, 'Now study this carefully...You may never see another case in your lifetime ....'

What that meant I did not know. Nor could I ask. All I knew was that a giant steamroller was crushing my body, as I lay in indescrible pain and helpless terror.

I've no idea how long this crucifying torture lasted, but as my senses swam back to the surface, I realised that somewhere, my body was attached to an intravenous drip, and slowly, very slowly, the cruel vice that had clamped every joint and every muscle, was made to loosen its grip.

Twenty-four hours later I was able to move again, and though extremely weak and nauseous, was very much better. Dr Audu, the senior doctor, in whom we all had perfect confidence, came to see me and administered half-a-dozen different injections. He explained that I'd suffered from acute calcium deficiency, very rare in humans, but undoubtedly the consequence of breast-feeding while suffering from severe diarrhoea. I was extremely lucky to have been within reach of a hospital and to have had the symptoms recognised.

Over the next few days I became stronger, although initially I could only take small sips of fluid. As soon as I could eat reasonably, I wanted to go home as the food offered was terrible and I was given no milk whatsoever, despite the fact that Baby Joanna was in the hospital too, and being brought to me for breast-feeding.

Five days later, when the usual bouts of diarrhoea were making me pretty miserable but I was still hopeful of going home, Peter arrived ready to take me and the baby, who had just had her evening feed. Starting to get out of bed, the sinister, cold, creeping sensation leapt back to life at the nape of my neck, my thumbs were pulled, involuntarily, hard across my palms, sharp tingling spread from my hands and neck all over my body and the vice closed its jaws again. I was terror-stricken.

Staff came rushing in and injections were hastily administered and after about an hour relief gradually returned, except that my legs remained icy cold and ached all night long.

Baby Joanna was brought to me for her early morning feed and after it I began to feel terrible again. I was increasingly certain that it wasn't a good idea to be breast-feeding when my lack of calcium had resulted in such dramatic and almost fatal consequences, much as I wanted to feed Joanna myself. I started to explain this to Peter, who arrived early, but almost immediately another terrifying attack began. Cold, helpless dread swept over me like icy water closing over my head. As my joints seized up, I was shivering uncontrollably and overwhelmed by waves of nausea.

Hurriedly, calcium was pumped into me again, the tetany receded but the bitter chill in my arms and legs remained.

Peter left, thinking the worst was over, but at noon came another onslaught. With more injections my body was loosened, but I was very sick and utterly exhausted. The relief lasted no more than three hours when yet another violent seizure began. Fortunately by now the hospital had prepared syringes of calcium, and I was treated quickly, and the assistant doctor (Dr Audu being away on tour) at last decreed that breast-feeding must stop.

For a long time I lay in hospital, unable to eat, taking only small sips of liquid. The seizures stopped but the biting cold in my limbs remained, with frequent icy sweats and constant fear, which was a physical sensation more than a mental one.

When Dr Audu returned to Kaduna he ordered a fresh course of treatment and X-rays. Very slowly I regained strength and was eventually given a short 'parole' when I was allowed out of hospital for an hour. What a joy!

As I tottered towards the car, there was Nicola waving madly and shouting 'Mummy! Mummy!' I had almost forgotten what it was to be a Mummy.

Another two days with short spells of 'freedom', then Peter was at last allowed to take me home – no longer in Kaduna, but at Shika, fifteen miles from Zaria, where we'd been allocated a house at the Agricultural Research Station. Peter had had the stress of coping with the move while I was still in hospital. Now he had to take over the bottle feeding of Joanna, but unfortunately she soon succumbed to salmonella which reduced her to a tiny shadow. Nicola too was frequently poorly, despite a robust constitution, and I was little use to anyone, with frequent relapses, but colleagues and friends were wonderfully kind and supportive.

❧❧❧❧

By the following March we were mending, and the baby was starting to regain her lost weight. Peter's father had written from South Africa, having had to leave Kenya in the post-Mau Mau era, and had asked for help running the small farm he'd purchased in the Eastern Transvaal. His health was too poor, he said, to manage on his own, but if we would join him, he'd take on extra land nearby so that we could live independently while he and Peter ran the two farms jointly.

CHAPTER 12

The Journey. It seemed a wonderful prospect, leaving Nigeria at last and having the opportunity of a real family life, with the bonus of land of our own to farm. Sad as I was not to have the chance of being with my own parents and grieving with them over the impossibility of seeing their granddaughters, the relief of being able to say goodbye to the frustrations, exasperations and unhealthy conditions of life in the wilds of West Africa was tremendous.

Our passages on a cargo boat of the Holland West Africa Line were booked; the car would travel with us, there'd only be a handful of passengers and we looked forward to a fascinating voyage down the West Coast, once the hurdle of the 700-mile drive to Lagos had been cleared.

Two days before the epic journey was to begin, we were ready to leave Shika. By 9 a.m. our loads, which had first to go to Zaria, were packed on to a lorry, but the vehicle wouldn't start: the generator had been stolen in the night. It took Peter 2½ hours to find a replacement, and the day's arrangements fell to pieces.

By the time we arrived in Kaduna there was very little time to gather the essentials unobtainable 'in bush'. To add to our problems, the shops had no disposable nappies and no tins of baby food. We needed medical supplies urgently, but were unable to contact the doctor until late evening, and had to be up again at 2 a.m.

Leaving Kaduna at 4 a.m. we soon found road conditions appalling, and for 120 miles we bumped and shook, dodging lightless, lunatic lorries which loomed up out of the dust and darkness.

Even after daybreak we drove half-blinded by the thick and choking dust thrown up by great swaying mammy-wagons which were impossible to overtake as they swayed like maniacs from one side of the road to the other, a mass of clinging bodies completely masking the outside of the vehicles. More than once our lives were saved only by a miracle as a lorry charged past on an acute bend, unable to brake. Many times these trucks failed to corner, and the tragic consequences were evident at the foot of every gorge, where shattered, dismembered vehicles, their entrails exposed, lay rusting in the blistering heat.

Reaching our first destination, Ilorin, in mid-afternoon, having driven for ten hours, we tumbled, filthy and exhausted from the car, soothing our distressed and irritable children with the promise of imminent comfort. Peter hurried to the reception desk, but was back within minutes, his face as black as thunder. 'She's cancelled our bookings,' he said. 'The place is now full of politicians. Our room has been taken over. She couldn't care less about us.'

There was no option but to climb wearily back into the car and drive on. The next hotel was 100 miles further on, in Ibadan. There, to our relief, we were able to get a reasonable room at the Rest House, and after a few hours' sleep set out for Lagos, having tried in vain to find a store where we could buy the essential items for the children that the North had failed to provide.

Now our route took us through mangrove swamps and across creeks busy with dugout canoes and lined with wretched bamboo hovels. Peter paused to take a photograph of a boat loaded with gaily-dressed women apparently on their way to the city's markets, but threatening gestures and shouted abuse made us retreat to the car and continue into the chaos of Lagos itself. On the teeming, noisy streets were crammed tumbledown slum dwellings with precarious tin roofs. We drove through avenues of abandoned broken-down cars, still dodging manic mammy-wagons which careered in all directions. To be close to one at a junction was ludicrously hazardous; a forest of arms would appear, wavingly madly, from both near and offside, and of the half-dozen potential manoeuvres not one was actually signalled in advance.

Though many people were colourfully, even extravagantly dressed, especially women, there seemed to be no pride in their homes. In Ibadan we had seen decorated walls, interesting window shapes and curiously 'eared' houses amidst the corrugated iron shacks. None here.

Remembering our arrival in Nigeria at Christmas in 1958 and our brief stay at the Ikoyi Hotel, we looked forward to two days of civilised comfort at the same hotel. Its appearance was as imposing as our recollection, but there the similarity ended. The room allocated to the four of us was tiny, drab and swelteringly hot without a working fan or air-conditioning. Two single beds had been pushed together to make room for a child's bunk to be crammed down the side. There was neither provision nor room for a cot for Joanna, and there was no bathroom or lavatory. The prospect of enduring such suffocatingly cramped conditions even for just two nights was more than we could bear, but the management was off-hand and unsympathetic.

To make things worse, the food was appalling, and we were very soon all suffering from severe 'Lagos tummy', which in my case brought on another seizure. Somehow Peter managed to contact a local doctor who gave me injections and various bottles of 'Mycin' to deal with our poor insides.

Our costs mounted frighteningly and, to add to our worries, there was no news of our ship.

A week dragged by. We tried Bar Beach once, but it was foul with detritus and the sight of raw sewage spewing into the sea via an enormous spout, plus the plague of teenage boys insisting menacingly that they should 'guard' our car, drove us away within minutes. Shopping could not be indulged in, as our finances were shrinking dangerously and the large, shrewd 'mammies' in charge of market stalls were more than a match for inexperienced Westerners.

Each morning Peter, more resigned and inured to difficulties than I, went to the shipping line office to try to discover what was happening to the *Van Lindschoten*, but only brought back increasingly gloomy reports from the empty docks where not a single south-bound ship was arriving. The only cheerfulness was that of the dock workers who squatted in groups with their Star beer, delighted with their unlooked-for holiday.

News eventually filtered through from Conakry that Sekou Touré, the Marxist President of Guinea, had abruptly nationalised this major West African port, resulting in a nautical traffic jam which trapped every kind of vessel in a web of chaos from which no escape was possible.

And so the days dragged painfully by. It was as if Nigeria, a great sluggish octopus, had only pretended to be sleeping as we rattled and bumped down that so-called 'highway' from the Northern Region, and now, just as escape was tantalisingly close, had suddenly snaked out one of its deadly tentacles which it had coiled around us, holding us helpless in its grip .... It was hard not to see symbolism in the one incident of interest during the first week of our incarceration at the Ikoyi: the sound of many voices chanting brought us out of our room to see a great funeral procession passing along the street. Dozens of white-robed, bare-headed men in ranks four deep, walked in front of a large ancient hearse which was followed by a less formal crowd of blue-clad women wives, concubines and female relatives all chanting rhythmically and cheerfully – in unison.

During the second week a snake charmer, decked in flowing green robes, entertained a crowd of awestruck onlookers, including ourselves, at the hotel entrance. (See page 107.) His basket contained eight or nine cobras which twisted, turned and struck at his command. One he held inside his mouth; two others he struck 'dead', with a 'magic thong' and tied their bodies in knots. After a minute or two, he untied them and 'resurrected' them with 'magic powder'. Before replacing them in the basket, he forced their mouths open and showed us their fangs. One he made bite his arm again and again, then displayed the gashes to our incredulous eyes. A hotel steward watching near us told us that a charmer has power over his snakes for six months only. First he goes to a witch doctor to obtain a special 'medicine', then he goes out to bush, whistles, and all the cobras in the area hasten directly to him. The 'medicine' makes him immune to their venom, he said, but it is only effective for six months ....

At last, in early April, the Dutch-owned cargo vessel, the *Van Lindschoten* arrived at the dock. Scarcely able to believe that the door of escape was finally ajar we hurried aboard.

What a contrast to all our previous experience! We were allotted two adjoining cabins, with a cot for Joanna and generous wardrobe space. The friendly Dutch officers said we had only to ask for anything we needed, and all the passengers had the use of the magnificent lounge, panelled in gleaming mahogany, as well as the sports deck. In fact, we had virtually the run of the ship.

Even so, the feeling of being trapped was slow to dissolve as we watched the lights of Lagos disappear, knowing that the first stop would be Port Harcourt, still Nigeria. We had a long haul up the Niger River, where numerous little villages dotted the mangrove swamps and small craft, like sampans, were everywhere. It was a sad and sobering thought that young children, even in the sixties, were being shipped from here to the Middle East as slaves.

The whole of the following day was spent loading iron pipes – surplus equipment from the Shell Oil Company which was transferring operations to Malaya. We watched young boys diving from dug-out canoes to retrieve pennies thrown from our ship, and bum boats laden with fruit, clustering round, their owners shouting up to us until a crew member let down ropes and hauled up a huge bunch of bananas and dozens of pineapples wrapped in cloth.

After a second night at the docks, waiting for high tide, we finally slid out of the river and, for us, the voyage began.

It was a newish vessel, the height of luxury to us, and offering great potential for risky exploits to our adventurous toddler. She was determined to dive off the deck rails into the sea, so the crew hastily erected a strong canvas barrier against them and produced a large, portable paddling pool where she spent many happy hours, much to our relief.

The females of the family were 'on the mend', as I doled out antibiotics to the three of us night and morning, and Nicola was as full of devilry as a wagonload of monkeys. Returning to the cabin one evening after supper to check that the Little Treasures were asleep, I was greeted by a scene of devastation. Face powder and make-up were all over the dressing table, where an open bottle of shampoo lay on its side, dribbling the last of its contents on to the carpet. The mirror was adorned with thick, pink scribbles from my favourite lipstick which had also been used to decorate the baby, who was blissfully unaware of the mayhem, bright cerise stripes all over her face. Her normally soft, silvery hair stood out in strange pinky-brown spikes, where a liberal mix of cosmetics and talc had been rubbed into it. Over her face was a messy goo running into the lipstick stripes, with startling white highlights here and there from the addition of toothpaste, which must have proved easier to administer than shampoo .....

The perpetrator lay sleeping beatifically, her own face scarcely marked save for the odd splash of lipstick, which had, however, been liberally daubed over the sheets and pillows. One sticky, chubby hand was flung carelessly up beside her still spun-silver hair, the other clutching the now-empty bottle of Guanamycin that I thought I'd put well out of reach.

My heart raced as I put my face close to hers to check breathing and temperature. She was very still. Anxiously I looked for indications of how much she might have taken from the half-used bottle and to my great relief saw a sizeable puddle on the floor, then discovered her little nightie was wet through. Her eyes opened for a moment and she gave a little humming sound, then slipped back into a peaceful sleep ......

The first stop after leaving Nigeria was Port Gentil where all day enormous logs were winched off the quay and lowered into the hold, some of them weighing as much as seven tons each. Timber is – or was – Gabon's almost only exportable asset, though we were told of a thriving trade in crocodile skins. An expatriate hunter had brought back two tons after just one expedition into the Ogoni Delta region.

Two days later we were anchored in Lobito Bay, Angola, to pick up sisal from the Congo (now Zaire) and copper ingots from Katanga. The port of Lobito was delightfully picturesque, as if it had been transported from Southern Europe, with its tiled pavements and cafés with tables outside under colourful awnings. In the south of the country the farmers were mostly Dutch, German or Boers, while in the north the jungle was dotted with coffee plantations run by Portuguese settlers. After Nigeria it seemed odd to see that it was mostly Portuguese doing the work – of driving cranes or taxis and serving in shops, for example.

Leaving the bay, the wind freshened strongly and the sea came alive with romping white horses. We tried to stand in the bows, but although it was exhilarating, we were nearly blown into the water. By evening the sky was dark and threatening and gales were forecast as imminent. A Russian vessel was pointed out to us on the horizon, gathering intelligence while thinly disguised as a fishing trawler, as grey as the sky, and sinister.

The following day started blowy and bright and we watched a school of dolphins playing alongside the ship and leaping across the front of the bows, but soon the weather worsened and fierce gales whipped up huge waves which broke over the ship with shuddering force. We spent many sleepless hours clinging to our bunks as the storm raged, and it was only later that we learnt how lucky we had been – caught by only the tail-end of a hurricane.

On April 17th we woke early and hurried out into the sparkling dawn of Table Bay. It was an image of paradise; rose-flushed peaks rising above silvery clouds, towering over the white, silent city. Fetching Sarah from the cabin so that she should not miss this magical moment, we watched the veil of silken mist slip from the shoulders of the great flat-topped mountain. Gradually the pale sky deepened to azure, and the water turned to gold in the spreading sunlight. The whole Southern Cape was shining, freshly laundered, from the snowy cliffs rising in the shadow of Table Mountain itself, to the wreaths of white smoke coiling upwards from all the vessels scattered over the bay. That this should be a part of the same land mass that had oppressed me for what felt like aeons, though only about three years in fact, seemed unbelievable.

'You can haf the day off,' said the Chief Officer with a smile. 'You can go ashore as soon as the cargo and luggage haf been discharged.' He joined us at the rail for a few minutes, Peter keeping a firm hold on the ever-venturesome Nicola, while I cuddled Joanna, thankful to see she was shaking off the pallor and peakiness of West Africa.

'Ho, ho!' the officer cried suddenly, with a big Dutch laugh. 'Look! Your big drums, is it not, going off for ever?' We joined in the mirth. Yes, there were several large blue oil drums identical to those that contained all our possessions, being hoisted off the ship with the rest of the cargo. But we were quite satisfied that ours were still tucked safely down in the hold, awaiting our disembarkation at the next port, Durban.

It was a day of delights. A hired car took us up to the Rhodes Memorial on the side of the mountain where elegant gardens showed off wonderful proteas, South Africa's national flower, and even lovelier, huge clumps of brilliantly blue agapanthus lilies.

On the peninsula the 'Twelve Apostles' did not seem awesome, rather, friendly and welcoming. Spectacular in the morning sunshine, they were laid out like a string of gemstones along its length, set off to perfection by the shimmering blue sea, the white beaches, the winding silver ribbons of road and the vivid emerald spread of luxuriant vegetation.

Cheerfully revived after an exhilarating day of exploration, drinking in thirstily the sights and scents of this beautiful spot, we re-embarked, tucked the children into bed after supper, then stood at the deck rails trying to guess the sources of the little blue clusters of jewelled light as the ship glided softly out of the bay and into the Indian ocean.

'Durban tomorrow!' we whispered.

We were wrong.

'No, there is no stopping at Durban to-day,' said our friendly Chief Officer the next morning. 'We haf to go to Lourenço Marques for unloading cargo.'

Mild disappointment was soothed by the pleasures of the voyage: in any case it was out of our hands, so we accepted the enforced extra week on board as a bonus.

I descended to the cabin to begin undoing the preparations made for disembarkation, but within moments Peter's flying steps brought him bursting in, and I knew instantly there was another crisis.

'They've gone!' he shouted, almost beside himself. 'Yes! they've been taken off! Those blue drums we saw being unloaded yesterday *were* ours! It wasn't a joke!'

I stared at him disbelievingly. 'But they were booked to Durban,' I protested, suddenly feeling weak. 'The crew *knew* we were going to Durban.'

'Well, someone's made a nonsense. The Chief Officer has apologised profusely, but that doesn't alter the fact that they've gone. Been dumped somewhere on Cape Town dock.'

Panic numbed me. All we had in the world was in those drums. After all the discomforts, crises and disasters of the past months, we had thought ourselves on the threshold of a different, more secure life – new home, new work, new country, leaving behind the ever-present miseries of ill-health and the constant threat of being tossed aside like unwanted litter in the uncertain political and civil climate of Nigeria. But the cycle of calamity was not yet over. Why us? In my darkest moments it seemed to me we were a marked family, doomed to misfortune.

Forcing myself back to a rational assessment of the situation, I could see that this latest mischance was exactly that. It wouldn't affect us immediately. Surely the loads would be re-routed as soon as the error was recognised at Cape Town? The extra week tagged on to the voyage might well be a blessing .....

Lourenço Marques proved to be an elegant town with expensive shops – closed for Easter, which was just as well. The only points of interest were the beautiful botanical gardens where we wandered for an hour, and the intriguingly grotesque straw hats worn by many women.

At last the *Van Lindschoten* turned its bows back south-westward, and on Easter Monday we anchored outside Durban harbour, forced by a howling gale to sit and wait for several hours before disembarkation was possible, then after thanking the crew, took a taxi to the Hotel Osborne, where Alice was waiting for us.

For four days Peter wrestled with officialdom at Immigration, Customs and the Shipping office until at last he was allowed to take possession of the car. Unfortunately, when it was lowered on to the quay the brakes were found to be useless and it had to be taken away for repair; I made the most of having mother-in-law to baby-sit while I did urgent shopping.

As soon as the Vanguard was ready we all took off for Uvongo, where Peter had spent much of his childhood. I'd never seen so many miles of glorious sandy beaches and rock pools, a surfer's paradise with wonderful breakers rolling in to the shore and graceful lagoons which lie smooth and peaceful beside the surf where hundreds of rivers from the mountainous country of the region run down into the sea.

Our fearless two-year-old was in her element and would have rushed straight into the boiling surf if not firmly held back: respect for the powerful waves only came after her father had carried her on his shoulders a few yards into the water. She was then content with bucket and spade on the yellow sand, where her sister was happily *eating* handfuls of the yellow stuff .....

After three short, glorious days, we left, threaded our way through the wooded hills which stretched inland beyond the horizon, and paused in Pietermaritzburg where Alice took her train back to Durban. Then up into the foothills of the Drakensburg where we stopped overnight in a welcoming little hotel from which we could see the famous heights – Champagne Castle, Cathedral Peak, Cathkin Peak – which beckoned alluringly, but resisting temptation as time was pressing and pausing only for a picnic at the foot of Mont-aux-Sources beside rushing, tumbling waters, we set out for Swaziland. What a joy to be driving along a 'super highway' after the nightmarish Nigerian roads. Little Nicola clearly remembered our experiences with crazy mammy-wagons, as every time she saw a truck she called out loudly, 'Naughty lolly!'

Never losing sight of mountains, we drove through Winterton, Ladysmith, Volksrust, Newcastle and Piet Retif where spectacular peaks suddenly confronted us and accompanied us all the way into Swaziland. As soon as we were over the border, the road surface deteriorated dramatically - not a good advertisement for a British Protectorate. At first the great stony hills were a disappointment after all we'd heard about this 'Little Switzerland', but gradually the landscape changed, emerald forests clothed the mountainsides and in a most beautiful setting we found the little capital, Mbabane, where we'd hoped to stay, but the one hotel was surprisingly, and unusually, full. The manager was happy to let us 'phone the next on our route, Piggs Peak, and at 5 p.m. we set off on the 50-mile journey, thinking it would not take much more than an hour. How wrong we were! Almost all of it required bottom gear, and Peter had to strain to make out, in the growing darkness, the fantastically devilish hairpin bends on a narrow ever-dropping, then ever-climbing trail. It was very late and completely dark before we found the Highlands Hotel and the little ones were exhausted as well as hungry.

In the morning we were tempted to retrace our steps for 20 or 30 miles to see in daylight the spectacular landscape we had missed the night before, but sternly turned our faces to the final 90-mile stage of our seven-week odyssey.

Deep pine forests obscured vistas tantalisingly hidden, but leaving them behind, we found ourselves having to stop every mile or so, gasping with admiration before tearing ourselves away to enter the next vast panorama of steep valleys, wooded gullies, peaks, peaks and more peaks, as far as the eye could see. We reached Havelock – the biggest asbestos mine in the world set high in its 'eyrie', with a twelve-mile overhead cableway stretching all the way to Barberton in the valley below, where the great buckets of asbestos slid down to avoid a precipitous road trip of 42 miles. Peter, who had spent part of his childhood in Barberton, told me that a mineworker had once decided to 'hitch a lift' to the town in one of the buckets, but failed to check the times, and the bucket stopped in mid-air on Friday evening. He was found when the cableway started again on the Monday morning.

The 42 road miles were worth it. Over the last four miles there was a drop of 3,000 feet into the valley where we crossed the border out of Swaziland and, scarcely able to believe that we had, at last, reached our destination, found ourselves in the little town, its wide avenues massed with blue jacaranda blossom.

So near journey's end, we didn't stop, but found the little road out to the farm, seven miles away.

Seven weeks to the day after leaving Shika, we pulled up at a little cluster of linked white-washed and thatched rondavels, and with sighs of relief piled out of the car. I stood back a little nervously, holding Baby Joanna while Peter, taking Nicola by the hand, went to the front door and knocked.

After several minutes, the door opened and Kay, Peter's stepmother appeared, apparently surprised.

'Oh, hullo,' she said, with an attempted smile. 'What brings you here?' .....

CHAPTER 13

'Dunduff'
nr. Barberton
E. Transvaal
S. Africa

Aug. 1962

My Dearest Mother,

I feel I owe you a fuller explanation than I've given in recent letters as to why we are moving right away from here instead of remaining with Peter's father and his wife.

Far from being the joyful experience we had anticipated after our marathon journey from West Africa, the time we've spent in the Eastern Transvaal has been a bewildering ordeal which will scar us for many years to come. Either my father-in-law's wife was unaware of his urgent plea that we come to help on the farm and his offer to arrange for us to rent neighbouring land, or else she *did* know (which seems much more likely) but it did not tally with her own designs, so she set about getting rid of us as quickly as possible.

The day following our arrival, which she maintained was quite unexpected, Kay demanded to know why we hadn't gone to Australia and how long we planned to stay with them! In the next breath she said a farmhouse a few miles away was available to rent and we should move into it at once. In view of her obvious misgivings about our presence, we would have been relieved to be able to do so, but we had no idea what had happened to our possessions, mistakenly unshipped at Cape Town, and couldn't move without them.

We suffered further embarrassment when it was made plain that the children were neither to be heard nor seen, but must be confined to the verandah or the lawn. The serious intent behind this 'request' became all too obvious when little Nicola's endearing attempts to go to 'Gwampa' with little offerings she'd found in the garden – a tiny flower, a shiny pebble, for example – were met with pointed indifference or irritated rejection. Naturally enough she became upset by the constant 'No, Nicola! Not there, Nicola! No you mustn't! No! come back!', but her tearful frustration, we were informed, was evidence that she was completely unmanageable. She committed a frightful faux pas one day when she staggered indoors with a broom three times as big as herself – 'to sweep the cwumbs, Mummy,' she said earnestly. This provoked outrage that a white child should think of doing a black servant's work.

I tried not to be upset (though I knew you would be, which is why I haven't told you before), and I can appreciate that small children can be an annoyance to an elderly person who has no interest in them, but I found it extremely difficult not to remonstrate, despite my reluctance to challenge anything said by my elders – you brought me up *too* well, I'm afraid!

Perhaps the lack of protest from me led Kay to think *she* could organise the children's lives, because then she insisted that Peggy, the house girl, should take charge of them. I reluctantly agreed to a temporary arrangement, but the very next day had to remove them promptly when I discovered the girl was giving them raw potatoes picked up from the ground to eat.

That evening Kay called me to accompany her to Peggy's quarters, saying that she was very ill and could I help .... ? In fact she was drunk! Paralytic, and her room stank of liquor .... Why on earth should Kay expect me to put our precious babes in her charge?

Peter soon began to have doubts about his father's attitude, too. He avoided mentioning 'partnership', other than saying in passing that the rent being asked for the adjoining piece of land was too high for it to be a viable proposition. When no alternative was suggested, Peter thought he'd better start exploring the immediate area for possible farms to lease, or else buy with the help of a Land Bank loan.

This seemed to cause offence, despite the fact that Angus (Mr A.) had stated categorically more than once that his own farm (miniscule in comparison with the one he'd had to abandon in Kenya due to sabotage and intimidation) could not support two families. We knew that anyway.

There were more ructions over the children. I was accused of 'criminal neglect' after we took them out for a couple of hours in the car to view some more land. Nicola had half-a-dozen chicken pox spots which the doctor had said were nothing to worry about since the attack was extremely mild and she had no fever at all. Kay, however, became hysterical on our return and behaved as if the child had smallpox!

At last our loads turned up and we prepared to move to a rented farmhouse five miles away. At this point Kay changed her tune entirely and implored us to delay our departure. To calm her, we agreed to stay a few days longer, but we knew her own son and daughter-in-law were arriving shortly from Kenya and we felt we ought to be out of the way by then. You'd have thought we could have sailed on calm waters for a short time, wouldn't you? But no.

It happened that the local vicar telephoned to ask if we would like to borrow their home when he and his wife went on holiday in three weeks time. I rang back, fully aware that Kay was within earshot, to thank them for their kind offer, but felt it would be more considerate to Angus and Kay if we moved into the farmhouse they'd arranged for us to rent before the Kenya family arrived, which would be in the next few days ... To my horror, Angus confronted Peter and accused us of being 'ungrateful brutes': Kay had 'heard' me tell the Vicar that we were being *kicked out* because of people coming to stay from Kenya.

We were flabbergasted, as you can imagine, but all my denials and protestations were at first refuted and then met with an 'apology' from Kay for '*repeating what was said*' ... We went straight to the Reverend and Mrs Lang and received their amazed reassurance that nothing I'd said suggested such a thing. In fact they offered to come to the farm and confirm it, but we were naïvely sure that now all would be mended. It wasn't.Angus simply stalked out of the room shouting that Kay was near a breakdown and I was making it worse! Just because I'm available as a convenient target for her imaginative inventions, it would seem I'm to blame for increasing her agitation.

I'm ashamed to admit it, but I find myself imputing ulterior motives to her, and she is certainly taking advantage of the fact that Angus is very deaf by misrepresenting whatever we say. Her daughter-in-law has told us that she is obsessively possessive towards her own son, so perhaps she harbours strong resentment towards Peter. I tell myself that her behaviour is probably symptomatic of the menopause, but that surely doesn't explain her antagonism. If she were open about her dislike of us I'd find it easier to cope with: it's the façade of charm and concern that is so sickening.

Despite everything, for a long time we thought we ought to remain in the vicinity in case they needed help. We searched the local area to this end but found nothing suitable. During this period we also had the shock of learning that Peter's leave salary from Nigeria was being withheld. This has caused us enormous embarrassment, and though he *hopes* to be reimbursed at some point, it's the last straw. We have no reserves here, and although Bill Curror, our 'landlord', has been extremely understanding, we've made the decision to leave. Peter will have to find a job in double-quick time, though I'm not sure whether it will be in South Africa (possibly Natal?) or in Swaziland. We do feel very uncomfortable in this country: the black and coloured populations are treated very badly, particularly by the 'Nats' (the Afrikaans ruling party), and I don't think we could stomach living here, beautiful as this country is.

I feel terrible that now I've opened the Pandora's Box of our troubles, the wretchedness we feel will spread to you, too. However, hope remains. I'm fitter than I've been for a long time, we've met many kind, friendly people, the 'cherubs' are very well and happy and we are living in spectacularly beautiful surroundings in this old farmhouse of Bill's. It shouldn't be terribly difficult for Peter to find a job, so there are lots of things on the 'plus' side. However, an unforeseen problem for him is that all posts require you to be bilingual, and he's forgotten all his Afrikaans – which he was never very good at anyway. (It's a compulsory subject in school and was the sole cause of him failing 'Matric', which is part of the reason his father regards him in a poor light.) But this is not a requirement in Swaziland, which is why he is considering job hunting there.

I'm sure I'll have better news for you soon, and in the meantime send you all our love and assurances that our spirits are *high*!

My apologies again for this miserable epistle, but at least you know the reason for our decision to leave Barberton.

Please 'hold thumbs' for us, as they say here.

Our fondest love and hugs and kisses from the Cherubs.

Penny

CHAPTER 14

The recovery of our lost loads was a huge relief, and although the circumstances surrounding our move to Bill Curror's farmhouse were so difficult, we could not help but be enchanted by our temporary home.

The house itself was roomy, an old timber construction with a corrugated iron roof and a 'one-holer' under the poinsettias near the back door. Surrounded by mountains and set in a green and fertile valley, it was an idyllic spot. The garden was quite unlike anything in our experience, bursting with colour, scent and luscious fruits of many kinds. We revelled in the novelty of oranges not just freshly-squeezed, but also freshly picked.

The children blossomed in their new-found freedom and in this healthy environment. Tears and tetchiness vanished and the serenity of our surroundings enabled Peter and me to review our own situation calmly, without our judgement being clouded by bewilderment and suppressed anger. We also felt sufficiently confident to add to our family a boisterous labrador puppy who immediately rivalled the resident cats in everyone's affections.

Our immediate inclination was to intensify the search for some suitable land, as Peter was fully determined to farm on his own account. To this end we widened the range of our explorations.

We were contacted by an elderly lady claiming to be an exiled Russian aristocrat, who told us she had a wonderful property to sell, or to rent, and her paean of praise was so fulsome we almost took it sight unseen. However, meeting the lady at the address she gave at Hantboschloop gave us pause. The house was grand, an encouraging sign, but we were escorted to a tiny, shabbily-furnished room at the back of the house where we were confronted by a grey, gaunt figure dressed from head to toe in black bombazine - Mrs Ladigensky, the housekeeper.....

Warning signals clicked in our brains as we listened to further effusions about the 'two big farmhouses, the wonderful position on the side of a valley, the lucrative store where you can easily clear £1200 selling goods to the natives .....'

Increasingly suspicious, we drove on many miles through sparsely inhabited hilly country until we reached, at the end of a rough track that looked as if it hadn't been used for decades, two overgrown derelict shacks on the side of a steep mountain that appeared to be almost all slate. There was little cultivatable land in sight, and the 'lucrative store' turned out to be a filthy ancient hovel. Its condition matched that of the tractor that she had described as 'in working order – except for a few stolen parts.' You'd have had to pay handsomely to get it removed to a rubbish tip. Her 'labourers' were in fact squatters, working entirely for their own benefit, trying to scratch a living from the few patches of workable soil.

The place was so wretchedly depressing that we quickly drove away until we were at a safe enough distance to laugh at our own relief, as well as the lady's ludicrous attempt at salesmanship.

A more promising proposition was a chicken farm, where the elderly owners wanted to retire. We were very tempted by the handsome house and big landscaped gardens, set in a beautiful valley. The only problem was our own ignorance about raising – and dressing – poultry. Too much risk we decided.

For several weeks we trailed round the countryside, wasting days – and precious petrol – investigating rosy promises which turned out to be run-down waterless expanses from which the owners were desperate to escape. We soon learned that successful farming in the lowveldt depended on a plentiful water supply and a frost-free spot, if winter vegetables – the big money-spinner – were to be grown.

At the beginning of August, our luck seemed to change. We were offered a farm in the Elands Valley that had everything we were looking for, and Peter set the wheels in motion for a Land Bank loan. We were on the point of signing the contract when, after a week or so of silence, Angus' wife telephoned.

It was this call and its consequences that made us decide that we must, after all, move further away, and led me to write to my mother, although I did not tell her about this episode - it would have been too upsetting.

Ostensibly wanting us all 'to be friends', Kay asked if we would go over to dinner at the week-end. I accepted the invitation on condition that we could find a suitable baby-sitter. This appeared to Kay to be completely unnecessary. 'They can stay *outside* the house – in the car – for the evening,' she insisted. When I – politely – demurred, and said I would prefer them to be tucked up in bed at home with a friend to keep an eye on them, this produced an extraordinary reaction, and accusation after accusation was flung at my head because I had 'no idea how to bring up children.' I remained calm, and asked her not to continue in this vein as it really wasn't helping. She was unstoppable, however, and abuse continued until I finally said, 'I'm afraid I'm going to have to put the 'phone down if you won't stop.' She didn't, and as her frenzy was quickly increasing, I quietly put the telephone down, inwardly seething.

Within minutes the 'phone rang again. It was Angus, summoning Peter to the farm immediately. Guessing that the reason was connnected with the extraordinary outburst from Kay, which he had himself overheard on the other telephone in the house, Peter drove off, braced for a renewal of hostilities.

It was worse, far worse than either of us had anticipated. I was 'a *murderer*' or would be if Kay 'died from a heart attack' brought on by my 'attitude'. A furious row ensued, until Peter was ordered out of the house and told never to return.

When he described the scene to me I wept at the injustice, the pain, the hopelessness of it all; then, drying my tears I resolved to have one last try, myself, to make Angus see the reality of the situation.

I failed.

Peter wrote to my anxious parents:

Dunduff Farm,
29th August, 1962

My dear Mum and Dad,

I've been meaning to write for some time, but the days have been flying – and life has been very complicated, as you know.

I was glad to read your letter, Mum, and hear what you thought about this awful business with my so-called father and his wife. I know the sensible thing would be to forget the whole thing, but somehow it goes against the grain to have an interloper, by a mixture of charm and trickery, succesfully turn my father against us.

The galling aspect of this sorry business is that no matter what proofs we present or how strong our denials, in his eyes we are a couple of rotten self-seekers, thoroughly nasty types.

Penny was so upset by the latest accusations that she went alone to confront him. He was working on his new tobacco-curing shed when I dropped her at the farm gate.

I'm ashamed to say that not only did he refuse to listen to what she had to say (which was mostly in *my* defence, as she is so incensed that my integrity is impugned), he even threatened to set his dogs on her.

She says the encounter was so melodramatic that any verbatim account, however unemotionally presented, would never be believed, and if it were a passage in a novel, it would have been dismissed as 'over the top'!

She still cannot face telling me all the details, and I feel terrible that it was my own father who put her through such an ordeal.

Thank Heaven the children are well. They're so much happier here than when they were 'confined' on the Barberton farm. I hope we can send more cheerful news about our prospects soon.

Love from Peter.

As disastrous August drew to a close, we had to put its horrors behind us and concentrate on the urgent business of finding a way to make a living. For a further fortnight we made an extended search for an available farm and *almost* made irreversible decisions about two possibilities. Closer investigation of the first revealed poor drainage which would be costly to remedy, and the second, which initially seemed to be an exceptionally attractive proposition, would probably have ruined us completely had we committed ourselves.

Peter had been contacted by a Jack Dorman who offered him a tempting partnership in a venture involving intensive market gardening, with produce transported to Lourenço Marques from the Dormans' farm at Badplaas.

The catch was that we were to be the ones providing the capital (which we'd have to borrow), with no guarantee whatever of its security, only Jack's verbal assurance that we'd 'get 50% of the profits'. However, the L.M. importer, whom Jack said was completely trustworthy, refused to sign any contract, and when Peter investigated his background he discovered the man had recently had his bank account closed for passing dud cheques.

Before the discovery, we had invited the Dormans and their three children to spend a couple of days with us at Dunduff. It seemed important to get to know the family, especially if we were to follow their suggestion and share their farmhouse 'until you've made enough money to build your own'. Close quarters' experience, though painful, was a blessing in disguise. The children were impossibly spoilt and their mother, a domineering, manipulative woman, would have taken us out of the frying pan into the fire even if 'the short period before you make your fortunes' actually materialised, which was beginning to seem an extremely remote possibility.

We politely declined the kind offer to make us millionaires, and Peter began to plan a fresh campaign of job-hunting.

The day following the departure of the Dormans and their fractious brood, we sat at the kitchen table pondering our near desperate situation. Some of Peter's salary had at last arrived from Nigeria, so we were solvent – but only just, and our options had shrunk. We'd not given Natal a chance, but even though his lack of Afrikaans might not be a complete barrier to finding work in that more 'English' part of the Republic, both Peter and I acknowledged our deep unease about putting down even temporary roots in a country where inequality, hatred and fear amongst the races constituted everyday reality. Divisions were not simply between black/white, brown/white, and black/brown, but also within the white population: besides the animosity of many Afrikaaners towards white people of British extraction, there were also extreme views among some sections of the latter.

So where should we direct our immediate efforts – Natal or Swaziland? Peter dug into his pocket and produced a coin. 'Heads or tails?' he said.

As always, I said, 'Tails'. And it was. So on the toss of a coin, the next chapter of our lives was decided.

CHAPTER 15

Swaziland. Two days passed in a flurry of preparations for a week's 'recce'. Besides dashing to ask every friend we knew if they had any camping gear we could borrow, there were also urgent arrangements for Joanna's christening to be attended to. Our unlooked-for return to England in 1960 had enabled Nicola's baptism to be a family affair, on my side at least, but Joanna had now passed her first birthday, and we wanted to be sure that Alice, as well as the friends who had supported us through our recent difficulties, could be with us for her christening immediately on our return from Swaziland.

We drew a blank in our hunt for camp beds until the very point of departure. Having been warned that *all* streams were suspect, we had to take large water canisters, and somehow a supply of tinned dog food had to be squeezed in too, as we could hardly ask anyone else to look after our labrador puppy for a week. Somehow beds and bedding, towels, clothes, food, cooking equipment (including primus stove), crockery, cutlery, nappies, toys (severely rationed) were squashed into the Vanguard and a small tent tied securely on to the roof-rack – until it all had to be rearranged when we realised there was no room for the children and the dog.

At last, at nearly noon, as the overcast sky suddenly cleared as if symbolically drawing back heavy curtains, we set off.

After passing through the productive vegetable holdings at Loouw's Creek, we found a picnic spot beside the Komati River famed for its plentiful hippo, crocodiles and tiger fish.

Soon the landscape faded to dry grassland, mostly browsed by huge herds of cattle. Immediately beyond the border crossing into Swaziland, a signpost guided us to the H.Q. of the Colonial Development Corporation. The houses in the Government Reservation looked temptingly and comfortably handsome, and after a long friendly chat with the Project Officer, Peter felt quite optimistic about his prospects.

As we left the office, a tall, strikingly-dressed Swazi went in. He sported an amazing guinea-fowl feather hair-do, brilliantly coloured robes, anklets, bracelets, earrings, library spectacles and a walrus moustache ...

The P.O. had given us directions to a riverside camp site 25 miles away, and we found it easily, driving through the water, shallow at this point, to a clearing on the far side where Peter endeavoured to secure the borrowed tent to the car under a shady fig tree. The children's mattresses were arranged inside the car and after such a long day we fondly imagined they would sleep soundly. Not a bit of it: it was nearly 10.30 p.m. before either of them settled, and baby Joanna was worse than her sister, yelling for more than an hour before falling asleep, no doubt as exhausted as we were, but both were wide awake by 5.45 a.m.

The puppy spent the night between our camp 'stretchers' (aptly named, as I woke feeling as if I had been tortured on the rack), but appeared to have spent most of it trailing all my reachable clothes around the tent in the dirt and fighting imaginary enemies with them. At dawn she proceeded to pull off my blankets and add them to the very grubby pile. I gave up the attempt to close my eyes and ears to the mayhem and got up.

The morning's drive took us through gently undulating parkland, green and pleasant, where herds of wildebeeste grazed. Several times we had the excitement of seeing groups of impala, one moment feeding peacefully and the next springing away more gracefully than the finest corps de ballet, their leaps more akin to flying than jumping.

We headed for Big Bend on the lowveldt plains and found a thriving district of cattle ranches, citrus farms and sugar estates. We had been directed to one of these where the owner, Jim Wallington, a confident, burly, twinkly-eyed little man welcomed us hospitably and offered Peter a job on the spot. Seeing his lovely home and obvious prosperity, it was tempting to accept Jim's offer immediately, but Peter had other contacts suggested by the C.D.C. office, and he felt he should investigate them before committing himself.

There was no shortage of places to picnic alongside the great Usutu river, whose waters were siphoned into a network of canals from which the vast plantations were spray-irrigated.

After lunch we continued in a leisurely fashion towards Manzini, but decided on an early stop when we found what looked like a perfect camp-site beside a wide, almost dry river bed. Immediately we began setting up camp, however, we were besieged by a herd of curious cows, half a dozen inquisitive Swazi children and two very drunk women, all of whom were very reluctant to leave us alone. Giving up, we moved further on and managed to settle the babies undisturbed. We turned in early ourselves and had slightly more sleep than the previous night, though the puppy would persist in yanking off my blankets, which woke me up half a dozen times. Getting up before 6 a.m. and feeling as if I'd spent the night inside a suitcase, I had begun to prepare breakfast when the Swazi children rediscovered us. This we could cope with, but when a garrulous old woman invited herself to join us, we decided to push on. Perhaps if we had been able to understand a word of what she was saying, we would have been more sociable.

At Sipofaneni bridge there were warm sulphur springs which had attracted generations of communal bathers and made easier the task of laundry for women who had no water supply at their homes, but years of non-stop use had caused the rotting away of the concrete walls and supports. People continued to come, however, and it was not a suitable place for us to camp, so we drove on to Manzini where we expected to find Balegani Ranch just outside the town. Calling at a store for eggs and tomatoes, Peter learned that the ranch was more than forty miles away, so after watching a Swazi customer stagger out with *five* bottles of gin, we drove out along a dirt road into a remote area where signs of cultivation were few.

Disappointment awaited us when at last we found the farmhouse: the ranch manager was interviewing elsewhere – in Johannesburg, in fact – but when Peter had spoken to the man in charge of the cattle, he decided the job he had heard about wasn't worth bothering with. We found the road to Piggs Peak, then made for Mbabane. Half way up a great mountain, we stopped to make camp close to the Komati River. The car radiator had boiled frequently on the way up, but the magnificent view was worth it.

The next day was Sunday, and shortly after making an early start in an effort to reach Mbabane by midday, we were surprised to encounter an African couple walking down the road arm-in-arm, dressed, not in Swazi traditional costume but formal European wear of a bygone era. The man wore a black tailed suit with waistcoat, high-collared white shirt and bright red cravat. On his head was a rather shabby top hat, slightly askew. His wife (presumably) had on a full-skirted ground-length green dress with leg-o'-mutton sleeves and a lace-edged bonnet tied with ribbons under her chin. I wondered if they were going to, or coming from, a church service, although we could see no sign of buildings or settlements anywhere near.

As we slowed down and pulled over to pass them on the narrow road, the man's legs seemed to crumple under him: he almost fell forward, but tucked his head down and went over in a complete somersault, ending up flat on his back, arms outstretched. Almost simultaneously the woman, in a flurry of skirts and petticoats, performed the same manoeuvre and lay with her legs splayed – fortunately demurely encased in long frilly bloomers – across her husband's.

Neither moved nor uttered a sound, but as they appeared not to be hurt or suffering – except perhaps from an almighty hangover – we drove on, uncertain of what to do, if anything. Rightly or wrongly we decided that, with two small children in the car, it would probably be unwise to stop as we had no idea what we might be getting involved in.

❧❧❧❧

Arriving in Mbabane, we wondered whether we might find an old acquaintance here. Athol Long, formerly Permanent Secretary of Peter's Ministry in Nigeria, had moved to Swaziland we knew, and this, being the country's administrative capital, might be where he was working. It was a long shot, but to our surprise, the first person we asked directed us to a large house less than 200 yards away. 'Yes, that's the Government Secretary's home and office.'

Rather overawed at the news of his importance as the country's 'No. 2', we approached the front door with some trepidation, but our nervousness was at once dispelled by his enthusiastic welcome and insistence that we stay overnight. There was to be a film show put on by a visiting American at the Swan Inn that evening, which the Agricultural Minister, Jock King, planned to attend, as its subject was a specialist aspect of animal husbandry. It would be an ideal opportunity for Peter to meet him and get something sorted out.

We were only too happy to concur, though doubtful we were fit house guests in our grimy state, but Athol cheerfully propelled us to the guest wing where we all piled into a hot bath and felt clean for the first time in five days.

There was to be a cocktail party after the film show, so it was a great relief that I remembered I'd stuffed my one 'smart little number' – just in case – in the bottom of the rucksack. When it was ironed, along with a clean shirt forPeter, and the children were tucked up in proper beds with someone keeping an eye on them, we felt confident enough to step out into the local 'high society'.

During a very convivial evening, the Minister and Peter chatted at length, and I could hardly believe our good fortune when I overheard Mr King suggest that Peter call at his office next morning to fill in forms and meet his head research scientist.

Deeply grateful to Athol who had really been our 'White Knight', we left early on Monday so that Peter could be at the Ministry by 8.30 a.m. There he met Tony Venn who gave him information about two posts vacant at Big Bend Experimental Station, one for cotton breeding, the other for irrigation and development.

'Why don't you go down to the lowveldt and see for yourselves?' Tony suggested, adding that he and his wife would be delighted to put us up when we returned that night. Such friendly and generous help was balm to our souls after the heartache of the past months and we eagerly retraced our steps. In mid-afternoon we found the Station, ten miles from the hotel where we'd stopped for a cool drink only three days before, and two miles from the Usutu River.

We liked what we saw and Peter found the man in charge of research, John Lea, extremely affable. If we came, we'd have the house nearest to his – not close, as the half-dozen houses all had very large gardens.

We drove back up to Malkerns feeling greatly encouraged and spent another civilized night in the Venn's comfortable guest rondavel. Next day, after more formalities in Mbabane, we drove back to Barberton and turned our minds to the christening.

Three days later baby Joanna was at last baptised, gleefully and noisily, surrounded by the little group of loyal friends who had helped us cope these last few months. There was a sharp reminder that the family feud was still simmering when Bill Curror mentioned that Kay had telephoned him asking if we had returned to Nigeria yet. She wanted to take over Dunduff for her own son and daughter-in-law and was not pleased to learn we were still there. 'Can't you get them out!' she demanded. Bill smiled. 'I told her the place was yours for as long as you needed it.' I could have hugged him.

❧❧❧❧

Peter's interview was to be on October 11th, and it was no hardship to get up at 4.30 a.m. and be on the road within the hour, the children still in their pyjamas.

The sun was just rising, catching the still-sleeping hills unawares and covering them with rosy blushes. The air was like sparkling champagne when we paused for a roadside picnic breakfast.

There were five other hopefuls at the Ministry, but Peter came away feeling reasonably optimistic and suggested we take another look at Big Bend, so the following day we drove yet again into Swaziland. The situation looked even more attractive on closer inspection, and while Peter's studies at the Royal Agricultural College had not included tropical crops, he was enthusiastic about taking up a fresh challenge, and gained the impression from John Lea that the job was his if he wanted it. The disadvantage was, of course, that the salary would be considerably less than that for his work in Nigeria, but that might be offset, we learned, by a teaching post for me at the local school. I had hoped to take the children home to England for a couple of months, but as the financial aspect was worryingPeter, I agreed to stay and apply for the vacancy.

Three weeks went by with no news from Mbabane. Our desperation returned and we began planning drastic alternatives. Just as we had begun to believe the tide might be turning in our favour, especially as I'd been called for an interview at the Education Office, we seemed about to be swept away by misfortune yet again. I telephoned to check the time of my own interview the following day, to be told that the vacancy at Big Bend School had been filled two days previously .... I was devastated. Peter was beside himself, and was threatening to withdraw his own application when the 'phone rang: could he start work in three days' time?

With mingled relief and dismay we began hastily packing up, realising that Dunduff had been our home for longer than any other, and that it was eight months since we'd left our last house in Nigeria. Now we must simply 'hold thumbs' that, despite this latest setback, the jinx on all our endeavours was finally ending.

As we left South Africa early on November 7th, I felt a great weight slip from my shoulders.

We were welcomed into our new residence by Constance Lea who brought tea and cakes across, and with them, bowls of flowers. Surely we'd be very happy here?

CHAPTER 16

The first few months were heaven after the hurts and anxieties of Barberton, and our living conditions luxurious compared with the privations and discomforts of our life in Nigeria. The house, our first real home, was spacious, cool and comfortable with a large garden where the children could play safely. The climate, though fiercely hot at times, was also cool and damp occasionally and never as oppressive as West Africa.

Peter soon became accustomed to an even earlier start to the working day: he was up at 4.30 a.m. and away an hour later when the children and I got up to enjoy the cool of the early morning.

Within a very few weeks I was asked to teach at the local school, and since Alice was anxious to come and live with us and wanted to look after the girls, I agreed, reluctantly. After the wasted months and expense in the Eastern Transvaal we needed the money, and the school hours were mornings only. The other families on the station were delighted as I would be able to chauffeur the five little ones who were pupils there and save them a long 'school run'.

The situation at the school was not an easy one to adapt to. The Head, an ex-WAAF sergeant, appeared to have no organizational experience, and operated on a very short fuse. While I could cope with her violent tempers, the children were terrified and understandably so, being punished for failing to get their sums right or being slow with their work. I became more and more alarmed by her actions and it was an enormous relief when she went on leave and the Department declined to renew her contract. To my great surprise I was offered her job, and with the appointment of a delightful new colleague there began a very happy, if short, chapter in my professional life.

Unfortunately as soon as the hot season got under way, my dysentery returned with a vengeance and I was at my wits' end. Luckily, term had ended and we arranged a consultation with one of South Africa's leading gastro-intestinal specialists at the Durban hospital. We took the opportunity to have a camping holiday for that week on the south coast, where relaxation and sea breezes restored my spirits and strength a little. However, the 'consultation' was farcical in the extreme. Obviously seeing himself as a psychoanalyst, the doctor asked me to remove all my clothes and lie on the couch. After an intimate examination of my body, he proceeded to ask probing and intensely personal questions about my marriage while I remained naked, vulnerable and extremely embarrassed. After half-an-hour's interrogation, he announced I was 'a nervous bride', and the severe bouts of dysentery were 'psychosomatic'.

I was devastated, and on our return to Big Bend went to report to our local doctor, an interesting and sympathetic character who had spent the last thirty years tending lepers in the Okavango Swamp region. He had been trying for months to find some means of helping me. Over that time I'd had fifteen different drugs to take, liver injections and a rigid diet of boiled rice and thin soup. Now he took up the challenge again with relish. I had to supply specimens every two days and he would let at know the minute he found anything.

Six weeks later he called me to his surgery, sat me down beside him at his desk, and with a triumphant gleam in his eye, opened a large tome at a marked page, exclaiming – almost crowing – '*Got it!*' He pushed the book over to me, indicating an underlined paragraph, and bade me read it.

'Strongyloides: rare tropical hookworm. Prognosis fair to grave....'

I read it several times, feeling slightly anxious about the 'fair to grave' bit.

'Are you quite sure?' I asked, scarcely able to believe that this hateful mystery could at last be solved.

'Oh yes. No doubt at all. I found strongyles – the hookworms in question – in the last sample you brought in. You know, they only show up once in every thirty specimens.'

He was like a cat with the cream, so pleased with his success after all this time, and I was quite speechless at the news.

'Now these should sort them out ....' He gave me a box of huge indigo pills, larger than any I had ever seen before, about the size of a humbug, together with precise instructions for taking them.

After enduring the misery of frequent and devastating attacks for so long – they'd started within weeks of our arrival in West Africa – it didn't seem possible that I could be well again, but within days, during which my inside seemed to have been dyed bright purple, I began to put on weight and to feel normal at last.

For our remaining time in Swaziland I had no more dysentery, although I did not know (and probably Dr Jones didn't either) that the strongyles were not completely destroyed. It was more than two years before I discovered that they had re-grouped and were awaiting their chance ....

Now that my health was so much improved, I was able to devote more time and energy to the children and to running the household. Sadly this created strains with Alice who felt she should have exclusive charge of both. When the situation became impossibly fraught she decided to go and stay with a friend near Durban and try and find a residential job in that area. This she did quite quickly and became a sort of matron in a girls' finishing school, which suited her very well, to our relief.

Routine on the Research Station was interrupted by the sudden arrival of a group of leading Afrikaaner M.P.s from Pretoria who used it as a base for a 'fact-finding' tour of the Protectorate, and whom we were invited to meet at a 'braaivleis' (barbecue) on their last evening.

It was a peculiar occasion. We sat informally round a campfire and had 'loaded' questions fired at us, individually, by religious zealots who were plainly not the slightest bit interested in other people's views, only in promulgating their own, which were entirely based on their firm conviction of racial superiority. When I tried to express a more liberal opinion, I was promptly given a stern lecture on 'God's purpose in the world ... He created men of different races, some white, to govern, and some black or brown, to be hewers of wood and drawers of water ...'

Aware as we were of the evils of apartheid, we found it extremely depressing to listen to these 'arguments' by men who controlled the lives of millions. Sinister, too. Their eyes gleamed with fanaticism as they warmed to the theme of their own self-righteousness. Having spoken out probably too freely, I had the feeling I was being mentally added to South Africa's 'Black List', and if I ever returned there to live, it might not be too comfortable.

One advantage of living in this part of Africa was our relative proximity to the Kruger National Park and to a number of Game Reserves south of Swaziland.

We spent a memorable day in the Ndumu Reserve, in the northernmost part of Natal close to the border of what was then Portugese East Africa. From Big Bend, we zigzagged around the Lebombo Hills making a journey of 65 miles instead of the crow's 30.

Signs directed us to the rangers' permanent camp where, on high ground overlooking a spectacular pattern of lakes, swamps and rivers, were situated three modern bungalows and seven rondavels (square ones) housing assistants and equipment.

We were greeted by a young ranger who was to be our guide for the day and, as we transferred to his Land-Rover, Tony explained that the problem of poaching remained at a serious level, despite a sizeable reduction in the local population, and necessitated maintaining a strong team within the Reserve. It was horrifying to listen to his description of some of the methods used by the gangs. A common one was to place stakes and planks along the 'runs' that the hippopotami use nightly when they leave the water to graze, having inserted six-inch nails along their length, protruding upwards and thus impaling the great creatures so that they die slowly and in unspeakable agony. All for the sake of their fat, sold as perfume at an exorbitant price. There were three hundred hippo left, about 1500 crocodiles and just ten rhino.

There was no shortage of other wildlife, and as we bumped along the myriad game tracks and in and out of woodland, thick bush, or across grassland dotted with taller trees, we saw nyala, forest duiker, several large groups of impala as well as many kinds of water birds and majestic fish eagles swooping down from high above the 'fever trees' which lined the water courses. And of course hundreds upon hundreds of crocodiles.

It seemed that they made their sunbathing arrangements with mathematical precision, as they stretched out in strict size order in a huge horseshoe around the edge of one of the shallow lakes that are a feature of this Reserve. From the safety of a nearby hide we gazed upon the awesome spectacle of these silent, sinister dinosaurs, their jaws gaping hugely as they lay motionless in the midday heat. All faced the water, side by scaly side, the smallest perhaps only six feet long, at one end of the near-circle, graduating evenly to the monsters of well over twenty feet at the far side.

While the number of tribespeople living in the Reserve had been reduced from 6,000 to 1,500 since its establishment, those remaining took unbelievable risks as they moved about, particularly in the rains, when even more land than usual was under water. The authorities had built wooden 'walkways' over danger spots for their safety, but these were frequently ignored, with tragic consequences, as the crocs picked off easy victims.

Hearing this made Tony's account of an incident involving a group of tourists all the more extraordinary.

About thirty visitors to the Reserve were being taken on a water tour as part of their 'safari experience' around the lakes in a flat-bottomed craft when, quite unexpectedly, a playful – or perhaps disgruntled – hippo took a large bite out of it and it sank like a stone in about 4½ feet of water.

Immediately all the crocodiles sunbathing langorously around the lake heaved themselves up and launched themselves into the water, gliding up from every quarter to form an almost complete circle, around the terrified visitors.

With incredible coolness, the ranger retrieved the end of the long mooring rope, extended it to a thirty-yard length by attaching a spare supply from his belt and *swam* through the gap in the ring of waiting crocodiles to the shore, where he climbed out and tied the end of the rope to an overhanging tree. Then he re-entered the water and returned to the sunken boat where he gently but firmly persuaded his terrified flock – all on tiptoes up to their chests, neck, or even noses in the water – that they *must* run the gauntlet of that gap themselves, via the rope that would steady them, as quickly, quietly and with as little disturbance of the water as possible.

He proceeded to shepherd each of them to the bank, encouraging and supporting those many who were on the point of fainting with fright, until, within fifteen minutes, they were all, incredibly, safely ashore.

To this day, no one knows why the crocs, did not attack. Tony suggested the possibility they were not actually hungry, the lake being extremely rich in fish.

Feeling decidedly shaky at being within spitting distance of the reptiles, I was vastly relieved to get back to the Land-Rover, but before we continued our tour, Tony related another story, admittedly apochryphal, but, he maintained, certainly credible given that superstition plays a leading role in the lives of primitive people. In any case, he had heard the gruesome tale from an elder in a nearby village.

It concerned a woman who, as she was busily engaged in doing her washing in the shallow water at the river's edge, was seized by an enormus crocodile, and while her family and friends looked on helplessly, was taken in these terrible jaws and dragged under, screaming in terror. Amazingly, she was not immediately devoured, but carried downstream to a kind of hollowed-out shelf in the bank just below the surface, where the beast deposited her along with the remains of his other prey – a revolting mess of bones and decaying f lesh.

Terribly injured, with gaping wounds, she regained consciousness and, finding herself in this hellish hole, managed to stand up and discovered that her head was out of the water and that she was, astonishingly, alive.

Weakly, she clambered out onto the bank and stumbled, dripping blood, back towards her village, sobbing with shock and pain.

Hearing her cries, the villagers tumbled out of their huts and stood gaping at the figure staggering towards them. When she fell, exhausted and semi-conscious, they rushed towards her, but merciful intentions turned to all-consuming fear when they recognized her. Less than half-an-hour previously they had wailed in grief as the crocodile took her; now they wailed in terror at this apparition from the dead, returning from the spirit world to curse the village for failing to save her.

'Send her back,' screamed an hysterical voice in the crowd, and the shout was taken up by the mob as they seized the poor victim and carried her, too weak to protest, to the river bank. Flinging her into the murky water despite her feeble struggles and protestations, their fear turned to relieved elation as, almost immediately there were a few moments of tumultuous splashing as a saurian brute – the same one? – tossed the woman upward like a rag doll. Then the cruel jaws, from which this time there would be no miraculous escape, clamped around her thin body and the brown water closed over her.

When this sad tale ended, we were silent for some minutes, lost in our own imaginings of life in a community hemmed in by superstition, witchcraft and irrational fears....

Leaving the lake, we headed up a rough track on the gently sloping hillside into scrubby woodland. After a few hundred yards Tony braked abruptly. 'Look!' he breathed and all heads turned in the direction he indicated. There, in a wide clearing, not more then 50 yards away, stood a magnificent bull rhinoceros. Holding our breath as this armoured colossus, who appeared to have stepped straight out of the pages of pre-history, raised his great head and turned it in our direction as if gauging our scent and the distance between us, we felt immensely privileged to be within the world of this extraordinary and rare creature, the white, or 'square lipped' rhino.

Gazing at the improbability of its appearance – the enormous horn on its snout below the tiny piggy eyes, the great folds of iron hide that drooped incongruously from its belly – it seemed all too likely that future generations might see it only as a faded photograph, a museum piece or an exotic book illustration, if the drastic measures to prevent its threatened extinction were unsuccessful.

The snake-charmer at Lagos

Middle Belt Nigerian village

'His eyesight is very poor, but if he locates us he'll be over here like a shot,' said Tony, who had taken care not to switch the engine off. We moved on, and I hoped fervently that our children, young as they were, might always have this living, awe-inspiring image imprinted on their minds.

When it was possible to converse in normal voices again, Peter related an anecdote about a dramatic confrontation with a rhino in the wilds of East Africa. A colleague in Kenya was surveying alone in remote bush country and found himself on a narrow game path with ten-foot high grass on either side, completely blocking any view of the terrain, and with no side-turning in sight.

'Jake suddenly saw a huge rhino, only about 25 yards ahead,' said Peter, 'and before he had time to think, it turned and charged him. Convinced that his end had come, Jake fell flat on his back and the rhino ran right over him, his horn lowered, and scooped off all the buttons on the front of his bush shirt. Otherwise he was unscathed, apart from having nearly died of fright.'

I looked quizzically at Peter, wondering if he was pulling our legs, but, catching my glance, he said 'Jake told me himself. It must be true: he was definitely not the imaginative sort.'

❧❧❧❧

My sister came out on holiday from the U.K. and Peter proposed a trip into the Kruger National Park where there was a good chance of' seeing lions as well as a wonderful variety of other game animals.

Entering the Park at Crocodile Bridge, near Komatipoort we were initially and unreasonably disappointed, as all we saw were impala, herds of zebra and a couple of distant giraffe. However, when Peter unexpectedly braked and switched off the engine, I realised something unusual was afoot.

He pointed to an area of woodland whose thinning edge was about 150 yards from the road and I realised that giant shapes were emerging from the trees. Soon a group of about ten elephants could clearly be seen, and as they drew nearer we could see two babies trotting comfortably between the huge legs of their mothers and aunts. The party was preceded by an imposing matriarch who, as she led her charges across the road barely 25 yards in front of us, paused and turned towards us, making us feel humble and insignificant before her gaze. For a few moments there were flickers of fear too, as she took several steps towards us, her great ears raised and flapping with the unmistakable message that we were trespassers and she the empress of this, her world. We sat quite still, scarcely daring to breathe, until she suddenly backed away and, raising her trunk, trumpeted loudly as she ran back to her waiting family, now safely across what seemed suddenly utterly incongrous in a land where man was an interloper – the tarmac road.

Finding the camp at Pretoriuskop too overcrowded to accommodate us, we retreated to the vicinity of Numbi Gate to spend the night, or part of it, as we were on the road again at 4.30 a.m. Even so, there were thirty cars ahead of us, everyone eager to be in the Park at first light.

After a morning full of delights, seeing three or four types of gazelle, plenty of baboons, several buffalo, more elephant, a rarely seen group of Kudu bulls and, my favourite, elegant giraffe, swaying gently as they picked their way daintly between the thorn trees, and if startled, moving over the grassland like rocking horses, lofty and magical, we picknicked (in the car) before exploring further. Still no lions.

Peter drove into a remote part of the Reserve and I felt sure that if anyone could find them, he would.

We found ourselves in a lightly-wooded area where the road narrowed and twisted around shallow hills. We were glad of the occasional shade, and Peter stopped the car so that I could give the girls a cool drink.

'I think I can see something over there,' he said quietly, pointing ahead to a small clearing blotched with dappled shade. He switched on, intending to take a closer look, but the engine snorted, stuttered and refused to start.

'Damn! .... and I can't get out,' he said in exasperation. 'There's definitely a pride under that tree in the clearing and it would be more than my life's worth to fiddle about or try to push. They'd be over here in a matter of seconds.'

By this time I'd managed to make them out among the shadows. There appeared to be at least three lionesses, a couple of half-grown cubs, and aloof and some yards away, 'Big Daddy' facing them from the shade of a thornbush.

For some minutes we sat helplessly wondering what on earth to do. We had no means of summoning a Park ranger, and we were a long way from the 'touristy' areas of the Reserve.

Just as we began to be seriously worried by our predicament, a big Citroën, the first car we'd seen for hours, appeared behind us and Peter waved and beckoned to the driver to come alongside.

'No problem,' said the cheerful chap at the wheel when the situation was explained. 'We'll get behind you and give you a push start.'

He backed into position and attempted to align the bumpers, but even with the French car's adjustable suspension, they wouldn't quite match.

'Don't worry,' he called. 'Mary can drive and I'll sit on the end of your bonnet .... that ought to make your rear bumper come up just enough.'

Before we could stop him, he leapt out of his car and jumped up on the front of ours, completely ignoring our frantic pleas not to take such a terrible risk. With a confident grin he waved to his wife. 'Come on Mary!' he called. Can you do it?'

'Spot on, George!' came the reply, and within seconds we were being propelled, willy-nilly, down the slope, directly towards the lions' resting place.

We held our breath as we passed within feet of the big golden cats, and as soon as our engine jumped into life, Peter braked carefully so as not to dislodge our Samaritan, and called softly but with urgency in his voice, telling him to come in with us as fast as he could, and we'd drive him back to his own vehicle, a hundred yards or so back up the hill.

'No, I'm fine. I'm happy to walk,' said George, again refusing to listen to our concerns for his safety. He wandered nonchalantly off, waving as he went, and we watched in an agony of fear until, to our huge relief, he climbed back into the Citroën, safe and sound, then promptly drove alongside us again.

'I say, I don't suppose you know if there are any lions about, do you? We've been looking all day without any luck and we'll be very disappointed if we have to leave without a sight of a single one.'

Wordlessly, I pointed to the group sprawled under the tree beside the track, and his face changed colour.

'You mean .... ?'

Lions photographed by friends who were quicker with their camera than we were
Photo by Ross Gray

South Africa's 'Little Switzerland

Barberton in Jacaranda time, East Transvaal

CHAPTER 17

The Great Strike. We had lived in Swaziland for barely five months when, for the first time there were signs of political unrest – and these occurred in Big Bend, only yards from the School.

The first intimation of trouble was the sound of a commotion which reached the classroom windows from the road below us. The racket quickly increased until, by 10.30 a.m., work became impossible. The children whispered nervously to each other and the braver ones craned their necks trying to see what was happening.

I could see only a fraction of the great crowd gathered below, and despite the gesticulation and shouting I could not make out much in the way of offensive weapons, other than a few knobkerries. However, when some of the demonstrators left the mob and headed up the school drive, I quickly slipped into Miss W.'s classroom to alert her to possible trouble.

She shrugged, obviously uncertain of what to do, and I was about to suggest telephoning the Education Office in Mbabane when the door burst open and her cook dashed in, yelling, 'Save me! They go kill me!' and flung himself at her feet. If he thought there would be salvation from that quarter, he was quickly disenchanted, as his employer turned on him in hysterical fury. 'Get out!' she screamed, and the poor man beat a hasty retreat, obviously preferring the anger of the mob to her virulent temper.

The children erupted in anxious excitement and I racked my brains to think of ways to calm and reassure them, while Miss W. stood staring out of the window in disbelief and indecision.

Tension was heightened when, within minutes, the cook was back with reinforcements in the shape of two workers from the nearby hotel. This time, Miss W., having composed herself, grudgingly allowed the three of them to hide in the small storeroom leading off the classroom.

No sooner were they concealed than a chorus of voices from my own class announced the arrival of a convoy of parents' cars. There was no opportunity to find out what the disturbance was about as panicky fathers grabbed their offspring and set off at speed. Very thankful to be relieved of my responsibilities, except for the six little ones I chauffeured daily from the Research Station, I drove as quickly as was safely possible through the fringes of the crowd, my small passengers pale and silent as we forged a way through, then whispering their relief as we found the road home quiet and empty.

Safely home, it was a pleasant surprise to find everything normal, with no evidence of any kind of trouble. It appeared that the focus of the disturbance was the huge Ubombo sugar estate, and more than two thousand men, we were told, had been brought out on strike. Their leader was not employed there himself, but was an agitator recently released after serving a jail sentence for raping a minor. He whipped his gullible audience into a frenzy with his rabble-rousing speeches, insisting they demand a basic wage which was, ironically enough, *lower* than that already paid.

The following morning the parents on the Station were unwilling to allow their children to go to school, it being so close to the scene of the demonstrations, and, as 'phone lines appeared to have been cut, there was no means of finding out what the situation was. Peter refused to let me drive in without reassurance that there would be no more trouble, and went over himself to try and clarify what was going on. He returned with the news that all seemed perfectly quiet, so, taking with me only two pupils, I went in.

Less than half the school's roll turned up and, although the day began calmly, our confidence was soon undermined by renewed sounds of uproar as hundreds upon hundreds of people flocked noisily to the nearby bridge, and today there was a forest of knobkerries.

The news of renewed trouble quickly circulated among the European population, and soon a line of cars appeared to take the remaining children to safety.

Now I had to face the ordeal of driving through the middle of the excited gathering and it was hard not to flinch as knobkerries and sticks hammered on the car, accompanied by shouts of 'Africa! Africa!' Inwardly I was just as frightened as the two children who cowered on the back seat, but there did not seem to be a racial issue at stake, and we did not hear of any Europeans, other than the Ubombo Estate managers, being threatened with violence. However, the jitters felt by many in the white community led to most of the women and children being sent away from the area, and our school numbers dropped dramatically until the end of term.

The Research Station, comfortably detached from the centre of unrest, remained unaffected. Within a few weeks Big Bend had quietened down, though there were persistent rumours that the Progressive Party was gearing itself to start more trouble.

Within three months the rumours were proved correct and the area was once again in ferment. By now the authorities had prepared contingency measures: the School was promptly closed, soldiers from Britain suddenly appeared on the scene and quashed all efforts at organized protest. The agitation died down as quickly as it had flared up and normal life was resumed, although there was a sizeable exodus of nervous whites, especially workers from South Africa who had no real stake in the Protectorate.

Apart from the period of uncertainty brought about by the Great Strike, our own future in Swaziland seemed reasonably secure. The girls were blossoming, Nicola before her third birthday swimming like a tadpole, and Joanna rapidly becoming a water baby. They adored having playmates for the first time in their young lives, and their self-confidence grew in leaps and bounds. Big sister soon

Preparing for the ritual of 'staves' in Geidam

Above: Northern witchdoctor

Left : Baboon

The village headman calls a meeting

Cow-Fulani women moving house

became aware of her status and announced importantly, 'I *not* a baby, are I, Mummy. I a Nicky!' At this, small sister sat up smartly in her cot and, very smugly, began beating her chest, chanting, 'Baybee! Baybee!' at the top of her voice. She was already able to climb out of her cot, and waking one night to find herself alone, Nicola having been brought into our room as she was unwell, scrambled down and snuggled in the dog basket alongside Jane, the labrador.

Perhaps because it was such a joy to be well, to be living a 'normal' family life in a proper house, and with very pleasant friends and neighbours, I did not at first take Peter's complaints seriously – until the thunderbolt struck and he announced he was handing in his notice.

I knew he had become frustrated with the lack of opportunity for advancement, but having been in the job just over a year, I had fondly imagined he'd find some way of overcoming the obstacles.

Sadly, his frustration boiled over into confrontations with the head of research, and the atmosphere at the Station became tense and difficult. As soon as I was offered the headship of the local school when Miss W. departed, he seized the opportunity to move out, and we transferred to the little School House with its bare compound in the middle of Big Bend.

Job-hunting started again, but not in earnest as it was plain he was hankering to get back to Nigeria, much to my dismay.

He did make enquiries about work in Australia and New Zealand, but nothing definite emerged, and travel to the Antipodes by sea from South Africa was difficult to arrange.

He knew his old department in Kaduna would welcome him back with open arms, but officialdom was proving an impenetrable barrier.

For several months he spent entire days writing letters to everyone, everywhere he could think of, or else, planning to drive from Cape Town to Cairo to fulfil a secret dream, he applied for visas from the countries along his chosen route. Perhaps fortunately for us, much of Africa was in ferment and most of these proved impossible to obtain, so the plan had to be scrapped.

My own fervent desire was now to return to England, to my beloved Cotswolds and my much-missed family, but this had no appeal for Peter. Seething with impatience, he drove down to the docks in Durban where he left the car after filling in – each in triplicate – forms for exporting it to three different countries, Australia, New Zealand and Nigeria. Then he returned by train and began packing in the desperate hope of receiving a definite offer from somewhere or other.

Two weeks went by and nothing materialised, but he'd insisted that I resign, which I did with great sadness, and now we had to move in with friends. Immediately he announced his intention of flying directly to Kano from Johannesburg. 'I'll sort out the paper work when I get there,' he said confidently.

I was in despair.

Two mornings later, as he was setting off to catch the 'plane with the help of a friend who was going home to Johannesburg for the weekend, the postman arrived with two airmail letters. I held my breath while he opened the New Zealand envelope. 'Well, the Agricultural Department in Auckland is considering me,' he said, 'but they're a bit late, I'm afraid.'

He opened the other – from Kaduna.

'Oh dear. Howell is warning me that it would be too dangerous to try and enter Nigeria at present. He says, "I gather from your recent letter that you are considering coming here on spec, and while the Department would be only too delighted to have you here again, I must warn you that your idea is *out of the question.* This country's relationship with South Africa is so bad that anyone arriving here from that quarter is being *arrested* as soon as they set foot on Nigerian soil. Sorry if this upsets your plans but I felt I must let you know the situation immediately..."'

'What now?' I asked, hardly daring to anticipate the answer.

'Oh, I'm still going on the 'plane,' he shrugged. 'I can't stand this place a moment longer. I'll sit tight when we reach Kano, and fly on to the U.K. I'll see what can be done from there.

With a sinking heart I held the children close as he drove off – to what? and where?

Else and Johann were immensely kind and understanding and assured me that the girls and I could stay with them as long as we needed to.

For a week I lived in limbo, with no idea of where Peter was or what he was doing.

Then a telegram arrived.

'COLLECT CAR. SELL IT. RETURN TO UK'

My delight at the prospect of returning home at last was tempered with unease about the problem of collecting the car. Somehow I had to get to Durban, and money was running short.

Else assured me she could cope with the children and Johann offered to take me to the border post at Gollel. There'd sure to be several cars heading south out of the Protectorate and I ought to have no difficulty getting a lift.

I stood on the side of the road in the shade of an overhanging tree, wondering what on earth I should do if I was unlucky, but my guardian angel was with me, and just as I was beginning to get really anxious, a luxurious Scimitar pulled in beside me and I heard an American voice asking if I needed a lift. Seeing a smiling family comfortably ensconced, but with a spare seat at the back, I accepted gratefully.

My benefactors, visitors from New York, chatted cheerfully as we sped towards the coast, and on arrival in Durban some hours later, insisted on taking me right to the door of a hotel not far from the docks.

I felt my thanks were completely inadequate.

Spraying the undersides of branches for tsetse fly, a technique developed by Peter which proved very successful

Rest during arduous survey work with Dr Glover on safari

Elephants at the crossing

Christmas lunch in Swaziland

Next morning I was at the shipping office as soon as it opened, and wrestled with the red tape that had to be untangled before the car could be released. By 10 a.m. I was behind the wheel.

With a sense of fatalism and muttering a fervent prayer to my guardian angel yet again, I glanced at the map open on the seat beside me and set off on the 300-odd miles back to my children.

Perhaps by now the road has improved and proper bridges have replaced the flimsy-looking wooden plank structures where I all but closed my eyes as I put my foot down hard on the accelerator. I tried not to think about the possibility of breakdown on those long lonely stretches through Zululand, across the foothills of the Drakensburg and the northern parts of Natal, aware as I was that there were no garages nor even any pockets of habitation along my route.

Amazed that for once good fortune had stayed with me, I reached Gollel just before the border closed for the night and with untold relief reached Else and Johann's house to find the children tucked up in bed and my dear friends smiling their own thankfulness at my safe return.

Next day a second telegram arrived:

'HAVE BOUGHT ORCHARD FARM, THEMELTHORPE, NORFOLK'

My reactions were a mixture of surprise, misgiving and optimism. Burying unanswerable questions and doubts, I hastened to make all the necessary preparations for departure, find buyers for the car and all our surplus possessions (most household things would have to be left behind), pay final bills, get hold of warm clothes ready for the change in climate, and say sad farewells to many kind friends.

A big worry was the future of Lady Jane, the labrador whom we all adored. But she had to stay behind. However luck was still with us and the friend who had driven Peter to his 'plane was delighted to take her on. Martin had come to Swaziland a year previously to join a team of hunters who captured wild animals for removal to safe reserves or zoos.

He solved another pressing problem for me, too, offering to drive us to Johannesburg where we were welcome to stay with his parents before catching our flight to London.

On June 22nd 1964 Martin helped me to stow suitcases and children into his Land-Rover, and with the temperature at 90° we finally left Big Bend. In the late afternoon we reached our destination in the highveldt, and to the girls' great excitement, found ourselves in the middle of a snowstorm. The warmth of the welcome we received more than made up for the unexpected – and abnormal – freezing weather conditions, and next morning we were delivered safely to the airport.

Only when we were actually airborne did I allow myself to believe that, finally, despite all the troubles and disasters of the last five years, we would have the kind of family life I had always longed for. Although I knew nothing of East

Anglia and badly wanted to return to my part of the country, at least we would be in England, incredible though that seemed.

I tried to imagine the property Peter said he had bought .... Bought? What with? and how had he found the place? Orchard Farm, Themelthorpe ... What a delightfully Arcadian name. Thatched, I wondered? Roses and honeysuckle round the door? And masses of fruit trees, of course: apples and plums, which the children had never tasted. How much land? Arable? Pastoral? I was still on a cloud of happy conjecture when we landed at Heathrow and fell into the arms of my deeply-concerned parents. They had scarcely recovered from the shock of their son-in-law's arrival, unannounced and without their daughter and grandchildren, and without any concrete plans for the future.

Our joyful reunion was cut short when Peter informed us we had to go straight to Norfolk to finalise purchase of the farm, so without a sight of my beloved Gloucestershire I found myself, with our bewildered children, whisked away in an old farm van (belonging to a friend Peter had looked up), into the wilds of Norfolk.

En route, I asked about our future here... How had he found the money? 'Got a 100% mortgage' was the brief reply. How big – or small – was it? 'Only ten acres, but a four-bedroomed house. You'll love it. Just wait and see...'

For what seemed like hours we drove round twisty narrow lanes, never catching sight of a signpost. 'I know it's somewhere round here,' Peter kept saying, while the children grizzled in discomfort in the back of the van.

Finally we arrived in a quiet, almost deserted village where we found someone to ask. The man looked up from his lawn-mowing and pushed his hat back from his leathery face.

'Thimblethorpe? Thaas jus' down the road 'ere. 'Bout three or four mile I reckon. Turn right a'ter the railway bridge.'

The girls were now fast asleep as we turned in through a gap in an untidy hedge and Peter stopped the engine. 'I think this is it,' he said uncertainly. 'Yes, here's the name.'

There was a hand-scrawled sign which must have fallen off the rickety five-barred gate (now missing a bar) that was propped open beside us.

Hastily I got out of the van and ventured a few steps down the pot-holed drive to get a view of the house which was almost completely obscured by a line of scraggy fir trees.

Now I could see it. Almost all of it.

I wept.

Wildebeeste in the Kruger National Park

Spurwing geese in flight

CHAPTER 18

For a year we tried to settle into rural life in Norfolk, and struggled to transform the dingy dampness of the farmhouse into a reasonably comfortable home. Unfortunately we were greenhorns on the householder front and took the previous owners at their word when they glossed over the tell-tale wet patches on most of the interior walls. 'Never in the same place two days running ... often don't show anywhere for months ...' I had serious doubts, but Peter had already bought the place.

We quickly became dab hands at D.I.Y., although it was depressingly difficult to fight damp that rose, fell and penetrated through the walls which were built of soft, inferior brick made locally at the turn of the nineteenth century.

The winter was made more miserable by frequent flooding of the kitchen, where the floor was a foot below the level of the ground. Coming downstairs on a cold, dark morning to find yourself paddling in several inches of icy water was not conducive to family harmony. Money, too, soon became a pressing problem as Peter was unable to find a job, and it did not take long for him to realise that ten acres of the heaviest land in Norfolk with a few tumbledown buildings would not support a family of four.

Hope flared briefly when he was offered a position in an international poultry-breeding company, and was told opportunities for promotion were good. However this meant starting on the ground floor and he soon became restive.

Within a few months he was once more applying for posts overseas and even declared himself ready and willing to return to Nigeria.

Just as his impatience and frustration at the inevitable delays peaked, he heard from Dr Phil Glover, a leading ecologist with whom he had once worked in Kenya and who now wanted his support on a big project in West Africa to be funded by the World Bank.

Delighted that his expertise was appreciated and needed, he jumped at the chance, understandably enough.

'It'll only be for six months,' he assured me cheerfully and I hadn't the heart to dampen his enthusiasm, although I dreaded the prospect of a second winter in that bleak farmhouse on my own with the children, and I very much doubted the accuracy of the 'six months' forecast.

By September, 1965, a year after our return from Swaziland, he was gone.

Fortunately for him, Peter's arrival back in Nigeria was problem-free, unlike that of a colleague on the same flight who was detained all night under armed guard because his residence permit had not arrived in time.

During the first few weeks in Kaduna, where he noted that, post-Independence, Government buildings had become shabby and unkempt, Peter set about the preparations for the 25,000 square mile survey in prospect. There was much to be done, not merely the planning and arranging of supplies and staff, but especially re-drawing existing maps, in which field he was particularly expert.

He reported gloomily to me that the cost of living had rocketed, taxes had risen sharply, especially on vehicles, and new regulations forced drivers to take an expensive re-test every two years. Ex-pats were quitting in droves, so it was as well that he was shortly to move to a bush station, Potiskum, which was to be the project's centre of operations. Kaduna had become a very different, depressing place, but the challenge of his mammoth task prevailed over mundane concerns.

Aerial surveying was due to start in November, but a 4,000-mile reconnoitre had to be undertaken first, at the height of 'the little hot season' that follows the rains. In the gloom of a cold, wet, East Anglian autumn I read with mixed feelings his account of enduring a three-hour wait in sizzling heat, without shade or refreshment, for a ferry to take them across the Benue River near Yola, more than half-a-mile wide at that point. The ferry had to remain static for a full hour after every crossing in order to cool down.

Mubi, over the border in the Cameroons was, at 2,500 feet, considerably cooler, but the land was desolate and infertile, having lost all its top soil through over-cultivation many years previously. Occasional flashes of autumnal yellow stood out from the scattered Boswellia trees, but there was no brightness in the faces of the pagans struggling to scratch a living: not surprisingly their expressions were hang-dog and anxious. They neither smiled nor waved at the white strangers – unusual for rural Africans.

Continuing their expedition, the men entered the beautiful hilly country around Rhumsiki, famous for its stunning inselbergs – naked pillars of granite straining skywards like space rockets on a launch-pad, hundreds of feet high – and looked forward to finding hospitality at the Government Rest House; unfortunately it had run out of food and all it could offer was eight tins of peas. Luckily there was compensation forty miles further on at Mokole where they found a splendid country hotel, where the Cameroonian owner laid on a five-course very late lunch – all superb French cooking.

North of the town the land was terraced and well-farmed by the local pagans, then dropped abruptly to fertile plains where yields of rain-grown cotton almost matched the best irrigated crops at the Swaziland Research Station.

They headed back into Nigeria through Gwoza to Maiduguri, and so on to the bleak, mind-numbingly dull plateau of Biu, which does at least have a bearable climate, but here, as for much of the exhausting journey, food and accommodation were difficult to find: the standards of service in Government Rest Houses had sunk abysmally low.

Immediately on their return, Phil and Peter undertook the first of many aerial surveys covering areas completely inaccessible on the ground. These had to be completed during the dry season, but thick harmattan from the Sahara frequently delayed and obstructed the work.

By Christmas both men were worn out physically and mentally and were to join a group of veterinary colleagues for a week's break at Geidam on the river Yobe in the far north, near the border of the Niger Republic.

Geidam is the meeting place of many trails from near and far, giving it an air of exoticism and mystery, with caravans of camels and trains of horses coming and going at all hours. The market is full of life, trading in every imaginable commodity: blacksmiths produce anything from tweezers to cut-throat razors, leather-workers offer shoes, bags, belts, high-pommelled saddles and other accoutrements for pack and riding animals. The scene has remained unchanged for centuries – the bright cotton cloths, camel-hair blankets, cooking pots and trinkets, guinea corn, groundnuts (from the Cameroons) big heaps of kola nuts, spices and charms. This is one of the most populous areas in Bornu, where prosperity stems from the unique phenomenon of annual dry season flooding of the Yobe, which enables second crops to be harvested, despite the fact that only 10 inches of rain fall here in a year. Large herds of cattle flourish and ensure the land's fertility as they enrich the soil with their dung, the nomadic 'cow Fulani' moving their animals up and down the country according to the season, obtaining free grazing and grain supplies in return for this service and for milk. Theirs is a simple life, stripped to the barest essentials. They travel uncluttered, the women and girls carrying their few possessions in big bundles on their heads, and 'home' is a tall corn stook, stalks spread wigwam-style, for a night or two.

From an early age Fulani children share responsibility for the animals and it is not unusual to see a couple of skinny six or seven-year-olds directing a scattered group of the big white beasts.

The whiteness of their cattle is a source of pride to the Fulanis, and though they appear bony by our standards, they are necessarily hardy to withstand the endless trekking to find reasonable grazing. Their great enemy, the tsetse fly, denies them enormous tracts of tempting country and causes long diversions to safer but possibly over-grazed areas.

Fulani youths, lean and handsome with smooth Hamitic features and stiffly plaited hair, like to prove their stamina and courage in an extraordinary ritual. Holding small mirrors in front of their faces they must retain a smiling look throughout a fierce beating with staves by their fellows, to win the admiration of girls renowned for their striking beauty, copper skin and sensuous bearing - very different from Hausa women, who learn their subservience as females in a Muslim household from early childhood, veiled and seldom seen outside unless performing domestic tasks like pounding grain or fetching water. In most wealthy families the women are kept in purdah even if, unusually, they have been permitted a Western education.

Paradoxically, the powerful Emirs, who since the nineteenth century have ruled the mainly Hausa North, are descended from a line of Fulani princes, their sway in a comprehensively feudal system unchallenged, even after Lugard took over in 1900. His policy was that of indirect rule, which meant that their co-operation with the occupying power ensured the survival of their authority.

The country having long been divided geographically and racially into three distinct regions, southern distrust (by Ibos and Yorubas, principally) of the numerically superior but – in their view – backward and inferior northerners was, sadly, a recipe for disaster, when, in the early 1960s, Nigeria was pressed by its well-meaning British administration into a unitary state. There was too much resentment and fear on all sides for any hope of successful integration, and the inevitable explosion, a complete shock to most expatriates, but not to many Nigerians, occurred at the beginning of 1966.

On January 16th Peter wrote hastily from Potiskum: '*Terrible news*! We are absolutely shattered to have it confirmed that both the Northern and Western Premiers have been assassinated! The Prime Minister has been abducted and God knows what has happened to him...' In fact Tafawa Balewa had also been murdered and the Northern Peoples Congress Party was now leaderless.

When Peter returned to Kaduna three days later, all seemed quiet, although there were a few soldiers wandering aimlessly about and the town was very much in rebel hands.

He learned that the attack on the residence of the Premier, Sir Ahmadu Bello, Sardauna of Sokoto, had been carried out in the early hours. All ten of his armed police were killed before he and his chief wife were dragged outside and shot. His body was unceremoniously thrown onto a lorry and transported to Sokoto for burial. The young Ibo major who led the attack threw hand-grenades into the house which was reduced to a burnt-out shell

There were no more visible disturbances in the Northern capital, although the Government ministers had all disappeared – rumoured to have been suspended and sent packing to their villages – leaving the wide avenue of their large new houses (nicknamed 'Ministers' Row') unoccupied and an easy target for looters. However, people were warned not to drive to Lagos where there was considerable unrest following the dubious outcome of recent elections. Gangs of dissidents in the Western Region were stopping all vehicles with northern number-plates and demanding money. If it was not forthcoming, the car and its driver were doused with petrol and set alight.

Over subsequent days and weeks more details emerged.

It was whispered that the day before the coup, Chief Samuel Akintola, Premier of the Western Region, had flown up to Kaduna to warn Bello of what to expect, but the latter refused to act, even though there had been strong rumours of trouble brewing on the political scene. 'If I must die tomorrow, I will die tomorrow,' he said.

Akintola returned to Ibadan to face his own attackers. Reportedly he put up a tremendous fight and very nearly escaped, but his fate, too, was sealed.

To the amazement of many, the newspapers, including northern publications, hailed the coup as deliverance from tyranny and feudalism and the corruption that accompanied them. 'Now,' they said, 'a new Nigeria can be built and there is great rejoicing in the land!'

'It seems pretty obvious that the Ibos have engineered the whole thing,' wrote Peter, 'and it certainly looks as though the election-riggers have brought it on themselves ...'

The situation remained fairly calm. A Military Governor was put in charge of each Region and the general consensus seemed to be, 'Good riddance to the old corrupt regime.'

Slowly the news leaked out that *all* army officers above the rank of major in *all* the regions had been shot, some brilliant and non-political men amongst them. Peter conjectured that the reason for this selective slaughter was to preempt any comeback on the group of young majors who had perpetrated the coup.

General Ironsi, now President, had himself been on the hit list, but was forewarned and fled to safety.

Police chiefs were not targeted and remained at their posts.

On returning from tour, Phil and Peter discovered a mysterious visitor hiding in their house. Questioning revealed that he was the Northern Region's Chief of the Air Force, and had fled with a volley of shots behind him when the mutineers arrived at 5.30 a.m. to eliminate him. Luckily for him, he'd managed to get access through the back door of Phil and Peter's house and had hidden in a cupboard until his pursuers gave up and left.

For six weeks he continued to conceal himself in the house, sleeping all day and talking to Phil all night, which was utterly exhausting as he and Peter were still working flat out. Peter gave the fugitive his bed and moved out, only returning for meals.

They found their unexpected guest a most interesting and intelligent man, Sandhurst-trained but pushed into running the Air Force. However, it was a considerable strain harbouring a wanted man and, eventually, when they were sure of a sympathetic response, they notified the local Police Chief who agreed to him remaining in the house until it was safe for him to return to his home in Shendam.

The new Administration determined to eliminate the murdered Northern Premier from people's minds as quickly as possible. A general order went out that all photographs of him must be destroyed, references erased and, Peter surmised, his name probably removed from various streets, buildings, the Stadium and the Ahmadu Bello University at Samaru. He had been an all-powerful and influential figure for a very long time and much had been named in his honour.

CHAPTER 19

Survey work continued, largely unaffected by these violent events, and as it had been obvious from the start that the 'six-month' timescale was completely unrealistic, negotiations were already in hand to extend Peter's contract to two years minimum. At the same time, a request was made for me to be permitted to join him, with the children. The news of the assassinations and unrest made me even less enthusiastic to return to Nigeria, despite my longing to be 'a family' again, but Peter's letters assured me that expatriates in the North were meeting no animosity from local people. His own problems in getting the terms of his extended contract settled were entirely due to machinations at the Ministry of Overseas Development. A certain newly-appointed officer put so many obstacles in the way that even the distinguished and easy-going Dr Glover refused to deal with the Ministry any longer and both men had their contracts promptly taken over by the Nigerian Government.

Once that hurdle was cleared it was arranged that we should be re-united at the end of March.

Peter, like most expatriates, was unaware of the tensions mounting in the indigenous population of the North, and his letters were full of calm reassurance. However, the new President, General Ironsi, an Ibo, was regarded with great suspicion, and since they had lost virtually all their leaders in the January coup, Hausa fear of an Ibo hegemony grew rapidly.

While Phil and Peter endured long, often fruitless or frustrated journeys in pitiless heat, battling against inefficiency and inadequate resources to get the initial survey finished before the rains set in, I, in the chill of late winter in East Anglia, set about finding a tenant for the farm and preparing to take the children to West Africa. The contrast could hardly have been greater: leaving Heathrow wrapped up in thick coats and scarves, we arrived at the little Rest House on the outskirts of Kaduna where the indoor temperature was touching 100°. It was a great relief to find that the town now sported a large luxury hotel with a wonderful swimming pool, open to the (paying) public, and since I would not, this tour, be accompanying Peter on safari, life might be much less uncomfortable than I'd feared.

Optimism took an early knock when, barely a week after our arrival, the vicious hookworms which Dr Jones believed he had vanquished in Swaziland, but which in fact had been quietly dormant in England's temperate climate, suddenly revived in the extreme heat and went straight for the jugular – or in this case, for my stomach.

Defeat was dramatic and inevitable: Peter found me unconscious on the bathroom floor after a prolonged attack of violent sickness and diarrhoea and I was carted off to hospital. It was very fortunate that we were not 'in bush' and that treatment and diagnostic techniques had improved immeasurably since

1962. The culprits were found and identified within 24 hours and a tough counter-attack launched. After a week's intensive treatment with a new and powerful drug I was allowed to leave hospital, and tottered weakly back to the family, where I soon recovered.

For Nigeria, however, there was an infinitely graver crisis poised in the wings. During May, as we battled with the usual official obstinacy, attempting to secure the allocation of reasonable family accommodation, General Ironsi announced the dismantling of the country's regional structure and the tinder was struck. Bitter and angry Northerners reacted swiftly and violently, having watched the new military rulers take over the palaces and the limousines of the people they had replaced.

In June, anti-Ibo riots broke out all over the North. Hundreds were slaughtered and many more fled to their homeland as Hausa resentment grew against what was seen as an Ibo-dominated government. In July, Northerners launched a second coup, fearing that General Ironsi who, despite his Ibo roots, was a moderate leader, was about to be displaced by radical opponents from his own tribe.

However, Ironsi himself was assassinated, together with all leading Ibo officers. Out of the ensuing chaos, Lieut. Golonel Gowon, a Christian officer from the North and previously Army Chief of Staff, emerged as Head of State, although Ojukwu, Military Governor in the East, was very reluctant to accept his authority. Expatriates watched and waited anxiously to see if the inter-tribal conflagration would die down and stability be restored. Most attempted to continue normal working despite the tensions amongst their indigenous staff, and the inevitable problems arising from the loss of many of their most able assistants. A few packed up and left.

For a few weeks an uneasy peace seemed to be holding. Awolowo, the Yoruba (Western) leader, imprisoned since 1962 for attempting to overthrow Akintola whom he accused of rigging elections in cahoots with the Sardauna of Sokoto, was released. Col. Gowon appeared to be making sincere efforts to reconcile the various factions, but he failed to win over Ojukwu. However the latter agreed to attend a conference held in Lagos in September to discuss constitutional changes.

The talks were brought to an abrupt end by the news of renewed and widespread massacres in the North by civilians and soldiers who were seized with a maniacal desire to annihilate these clever Easterners seen, quite rightly, to be holding almost all the important posts in that vast region. Repressed hatred and envy were unleashed and spread like wildfire, leaving no part untouched.

In Kaduna, Europeans – themselves threatened with violent retribution when they rushed to the railway station to ease the suffering of many thousands of terror-stricken Ibos waiting in physical and mental agony for trains or other transport away from the killing fields – were made to witness in cruel impotence a never-ending stream of unspeakable human misery. It was unbelievable that the dignified, smiling Hausas of our experience (whom Peter had compared favourably with all the other African tribespeople he'd ever encountered) could instantly cast off the veneer of 'civilised humanity' and be transformed into vengeful killers who not only showed no mercy themselves, but fiercely prevented anyone else from giving even the most basic humanitarian aid.

The first-hand descriptions we had of these poor refugees were too harrowing to hear without being overwhelmed with despair and grief for their suffering. Many were scarcely more than living corpses; the mutilations, unstaunched wounds, sepsis, dehydration, shock, the haunted faces of mothers carrying bloody bowls containing pathetic fragments of their murdered children ... a nightmare from which the only escape for many was death.

Throughout the North, expatriates were forced to stand by, helpless and horror-struck as their house servants, often of long-standing and regarded as part of the family, were pursued and pitilessly butchered by rampaging mobs. Some managed to conceal the intended victims, and at great risk to themselves, bluffed the gangs into believing that the birds had flown: then there was the consequent problem of somehow getting them back to the East past hastily-erected roadblocks and Army checkpoints.

There were very many unsung stories of heroism on the part of Europeans who put their own lives on the line to protect and succour fellow human beings.

❧❧❧❧

In Kaduna, army lorries packed with silent prisoners, hands tied behind, rattled out of town with gun-toting soldiers in their wake. One morning we found ourselves on a route frequently used by the military and were stopped at a roadblock. After searching the car, the soldier on duty ordered us to remain where we were until permission was given for us to move. After about ten minutes a convoy of packed lorries rumbled by, followed by several Jeeps full of armed men. Shivering, despite the heat, we waited for a further half-hour or so, then the empty lorries, rattling and swinging over the rutted road, headed past us back to Kaduna. A few minutes later we were given permission to move on, and Peter, giving the two or three cars behind us the chance to overtake, slowed beside thick woodland, then making sure we were not being watched, turned off the road down a track beaten flat by heavy tyres. 'Wait here. I shan't be a minute. I want to see ...'

'For heaven's sake!' I whispered frantically, terrified that guards would be left to deter inquisitive visitors to the area. And I had a very good idea of what form that deterrence would take...

'I *must* see with my own eyes,' he muttered and left us, disappearing between the trees where I could see the lush wet-season grass had been trampled by so many feet that there were patches where the muddy earth showed through.

The children must have sensed the tension in the car as I fought to suppress my panicky fear.

'Where's Daddy going?' asked Nicola, somewhat tearfully.

While I was rehearsing a comforting reply he came running back and was in the driver's seat and the engine started before more questions could be asked.

We were back on the road and several miles further on when he said in low, matter-of-fact tones, 'Yes. All the evidence was there. The bodies have been very hastily covered up. There are still bits of clothing lying about and one or two spades left behind. There's a big clearing in there. All trampled.'

I didn't ask any more details. I felt sick. Luckily the girls were absorbed in their own games in the back of the car.

Far worse for many expatriates, was having to face the raging mobs. Bukuru, ten miles from Jos, was the scene of horrific slaughter and destruction and the small community of Vom, only six miles away, became increasingly alarmed at the reports of the spreading violence.

Tom Leach, the Director of N.I.T.R. (the Nigerian Institute for Trypanosomiasis Research), was on a routine visit from Kaduna to the laboratories there. The Institute and the Federal Department for Veterinary Research, which shared the station, were the reason for Vom's existence and gave employment to a large number of Ibos as technicians, as well as artisans and domestic servants, and so were an obvious and vulnerable target for the blood-crazed Hausa gangs.

The morning following Tom's arrival, the Institute's Administrative Assistant, Gordon Brind, returned post-haste from a visit to Bukuru with a terrifying account of what was happening there and a warning that he had seen bands of armed men coming in the direction of Vom. Immediately all the Ibos on the station sought permission to leave, then fled to hide wherever they could find cover – in culverts or patches of thick bush, while the Europeans waited helplessly for the attack. Tom's urgent calls to the Police Station in Jos were fruitless: they already had more on their hands than they could cope with.

At midday the leaders of the gangs ran into the Station, shrieking and brandishing pangas and staves, and set about the destruction of all the Ibos they could find, and their property. Safe refuge was well-nigh impossible to find in that flat landscape – Vom is situated around an ancient volcanic crater – and victims were hauled out of their inadequate hiding places, beaten to death, and often horribly mutilated.

The carnage continued until dark and was resumed at first light, by which time a few fortunates had managed to escape to the comparative safety of Jos. These included the Director of the Federal Department of Veterinary Research, Dr Ezebuiro, himself an Ibo, whose house was sacked, but who took the enormous risk of returning in the hope of salvaging some of his possessions. Providentially he was spotted by one of the European staff before the Hausas got hold of him, and was smuggled back to Jos on the floor of his rescuer's car.

On the evening of the first day, news came that a company of troops had reached Bukuru, so very early next morning Tom drove over to see the officer-in-charge, in the hope of enlisting aid for Vom. He was spared eight men and a lorry and, as soon as they reached the circular road around the crater's edge, Tom split the group so that they could each cover half its length and meet at the far side, which they did, having dealt with groups of insurgents en route. Then they moved into the Station itself, rooting out rioters still skulking in gardens and the grounds of the various laboratories, who mostly fled at the sight of the soldiers. Once or twice they met recalcitrant groups, but primitive weapons were no match for rifles and within a few hours comparative peace was restored, although out in the bush, the pursuits and killings went on.

During the clearing operations, Tom came across one of the few artisans who had actually escaped the massacre the previous day but who had rashly returned, hoping to retrieve a case of his few belongings. He appealed to the Director for help, so he, like Dr Ezebuiro, had to be spirited back to Jos lying on the floor of Tom's station wagon hidden under a blanket and clutching his precious case. Several times on the journey they passed stragglers from the attacking rabble, luckily on foot, so Tom was able to speed through them in a cloud of dust. Once an army patrol waved them down – tricky, as not all troops were disciplined and refrained from joining in the general mayhem – however, their luck held, and seeing apparently a lone European, they let him through without a search.

Having deposited his passenger with other fugitives in Jos, Tom hurried back to Vom where a further search of the grounds of the N.I.T.R. laboratories revealed a number of bodies lying scattered among the shrubs and trees. Alerted by faint groans, he found three Ibos lying close together on a path near the buildings. They were hardly alive and covered in blood from panga wounds. The cheek of one man had been sliced open, revealing his tongue through the gaping hole.

With the help of other staff, Tom gently lifted the three men onto the back of a W.A.I.T.R. pick-up, and drove as fast as he dared to the nearest Mission hospital, where they were quickly transferred to stretchers and taken for emergency surgery – too late, sadly, for the carpenter, who died from loss of blood. The other two amazingly survived, although they never fully recovered from their wounds.

Early on the morning of the previous day, Dr Ross Gray who was in charge of the N.I.T.R laboratories, had kissed his wife and baby daughter before leaving for work.

Both he and Maureen were feeling apprehensive, having heard rumours from Bukuru that this was to be the day of the start of the reprisals. They were especially worried for Kevin their Ibo cook who to their concern had returned the day before from visiting his sick father in the South in spite of the fact that when the rumours had first started they had sent his wife and children to join him and told them to tell him not to return. Ross gave him money and told him to get out of Vom and the North immediately,

At first all seemed quietly normal, but within an hour Maureen became aware of a rapidly increasing commotion outside and as she gathered up baby Katherine to see what was happening there was a loud knocking at the back door. There she found Yato, the Birom gardener facing an ugly rabble of some several hundred men, armed with spears and bows and arrows as if they were going on a hunting party. The leader greeted her formally and then asked where Kevin was. She explained that he had left the previous day. Yato backed up what she said and eventually the mob left without searching the house.

Ross, who was told that his house was surrounded by an angry crowd, returned home just as they were leaving and while he searched the house to make sure no one had come in, Maureen watched the mob from the bedroom window, hunting the surrounding bush not for animals but for Ibos. During his search, Ross found Kevin with his sister hiding in an understair cupboard. Kevin had taken the key to the French windows and when he found he couldn't get transport back to the South had returned to the house in the night with his sister.

Ross immediately took Maureen and the baby to the home of Jeremy and Di Roberts, who had only Birom servants, in case the mob returned. Kevin and his sister remained under the stairs until the killing stopped.

Kevin got safely back to the South, but returned to Vom very soon after the civil war ended. However, he found it so changed that he decided not to stay.

CHAPTER 20

While these terrible scenes were being enacted all over the North, we had no alternative but to try and carry on as normally as possible. As a family, housing was our immediate and pressing concern, but the head of the Tsetse Division, seething over Peter's reappearance and, worse, his semi-independent status as an expert working with the renowned Dr Glover on this World Bank project, tried to make life as difficult for him as possible. Unfortunately Dr Wilson had died the previous year, so there was no official help in the veterinary quarter that he could seek, but the British Council stepped in and insisted that we should have reasonable accommodation.

Grudgingly we were allowed to make use of the house of a senior officer for a few weeks while he was on leave, but we were abruptly told to move out more than a month before the family were due to return. Three alternatives were presented, all of them tiny, dark and dingy, but Peter was told he must accept one of them within *three hours*! An urgent plea to the British Council produced immediate results and to our amazement we learned we had been allocated one of the grand houses in 'Ministers' Row'.

Wondering if it would be a better proposition than the others, or whether it was yet another example of M.'s malice, we went to have a look at No. 16 Nassarawa – 'The Place of Victoria's People' in translation.

First sight was not encouraging. All the houses had been abandoned when their occupants were sent packing at the time of the first coup, so had remained empty for months. The curved drive brought us to the impressively pillared entrance where we waited for the P.W.D. Superintendent to show us round.

Understandably, the grounds of about three-quarters of an acre were overgrown and neglected, but I felt it would not need a great deal of work to get them into shape.

I did not know then about the goats, the donkeys and the people from the sabon gari who regarded the garden as a short cut to the town. And we had no idea that the 'women's quarters' behind the house were to be let, and the trouble *that* would cause .....

We walked round behind the house – almost a stately home from its size, though looking exactly like a blown-up version of the Abbey National house so popular on private estates built in Britain in the early sixties. These mansions were less than two years old, we understood.

There was a long narrow construction like a covered passage built out from the back of the house which, after eighty-odd yards, ended in an enclosed compound consisting of small flat-roofed rooms clustered around a central open space.

We were surveying this with interest when the sound of tyres scrunching on gravel told us that the P.W.D. man had arrived. A sweaty, harassed-looking individual, he introduced himself as Bob Carter.

'You don't have to worry about this bit, luckily for you,' he said, waving towards the peculiarly designed extension, 'but it'll be another headache for me. It's the wives' quarters. Each of the four had her own room opening on to the courtyard in the middle where they had their fire and did their cooking and so on.... That long bit is the passage – completely enclosed of course – linking up to the big house where the lord and master lived.' He grinned. 'I don't know what the signal was to let them know which wife was wanted. This place had a bell system as far as I remember.' We exchanged glances, thinking the same thoughts – what ribbing we would be in for once our friends and colleagues heard about this...!

As we returned to the front, Mr Carter's tone suggested he thought we ought to be prepared.

'I'm afraid we haven't been able to give these places much protection from teef-men,' he said. The way he shrugged his shoulders as he pulled a bunch of keys from his pocket told us that he was conceding in advance that the interior was probably not all it should be.

He turned the key to let us in, but the door swung open at the first slight pressure: the lock had been gouged out. He sucked in air between closed teeth. 'Oh dear,' he said. Then, as if a fresh idea had leapt into his mind, he suddenly turned to Peter and smiled broadly. 'Since you won't be able to lock up when you come out, you may as well go round by yourselves!'

Pushing the keys back into the pocket of his khaki shorts, he went quickly to his own vehicle. 'Be in touch!' he called cheerily as he drove off. Very fast.

'Heavens! Terrazzo floors!' I exclaimed as we tiptoed gingerly through the large, empty entrance hall. 'Yes,' said Peter. 'Apparently there was wonderful teak parquet laid everywhere, but the wives lit fires on it to do their traditional cooking, so it all had to be replaced within weeks.'

'Don't say there isn't a kitchen!' I began to feel panicky.

'There'll be a kitchen all right,' he assured me. 'The thing was, the women had never seen electric cookers before, and so they lit fires *inside* the ovens, and couldn't understand why the food on top didn't cook. So of course they went back to the way they know best. Look at this!' He was peering into an adjacent room where stood a once magnificent dining table, seating twelve comfortably, but completely ruined, its surface blackened and pitted from end to end.

'I can guess what's caused that,' I said. There were scorch marks and burn holes on our ironing board, as well as in clothes and linen. 'Charcoal irons, what's the betting?'

'Oh, absolutely,' said Peter, 'but I suspect they thought it had been specially provided for that purpose. You won't find many women's quarters with dining tables.'

There was no other furniture in the room, and the walls were as filthy and stained as the floor, so we turned back to the big reception room. Such furniture as there was seemed hardly to have befitted the official residence of an important politician. A large sofa pushed into a corner had a couple of springs dangling to the floor at one end and its cover, like those of the four armchairs scattered round the room, was torn and dirty.

'It'll be difficult to arrange furniture in here, although the room's so big,' I said. 'It seems odd to have doors in the middle of every wall: I wonder where they lead to?... *ugh*!' I pushed one open and immediately shrank back, clamping my hands over my nose and mouth.

'Oh my God!' Peter, too, covered his nose. 'How on earth did they manage that!' he exclaimed, pointing to the ceiling.

The open door revealed what we eventually perceived to be a large cloak-room, but it was some moments before we could take in what was under that disgusting encrusted mess, plastered not only over the whole of the lavatory, the wash basin and the floor but also all the way up the walls and overhead.

I backed away. 'Well, let's try the other two doors,' and gingerly I opened one then shut it quickly. 'Same again, I'm afraid.'

Peter said, 'The third must go somewhere different, there can't be three all leading off this room.' But there were. The last was bigger, with a bath, but was in as revolting a state as the others.

'Let's go,' I said, 'I don't want to see any more.'

'It'll all be cleaned up before we move in,' said Peter reassuringly. 'They'll have to do a big restoration job: look, all the light fittings, switches even, have been pulled out of the walls.'

I sighed. 'Let's have a quick look upstairs then, but I dread to think what we'll find.'

We climbed the wide stairway, which must have been quite superb when the house was first finished, and to our surprise found only two bedrooms, both enormous, either side of a landing the size of an average sitting room. There was yet another bathroom on this floor, fortunately in a better state than the ones downstairs.

'That reception room was where the big shot did all his entertaining of the hangers-on, the toadies, the numerous dependants,' Peter explained. 'I expect quite a lot of them lived here more or less permanently. But of course no women or children. They all stayed in those separate quarters we saw.'

In the larger of the bedrooms I was puzzled to see what looked like a large wardrobe, but instead of doors, sheets of chicken wire had been roughly nailed across, and one side pulled back. 'What on earth...?' I peered through the mesh and the mystery was solved: dingy white feathers were scattered over the wardrobe floor, and bending the netting back I could make out dessicated droppings underneath them.

'Good Lord!' Peter laughed. 'That's a first! Inventive I have to admit.' 'But where did he keep his clothes?' I wanted to know. 'Robes are laid flat in a chest ... yes, there it is.' He pointed to a large wooden box on the far side of the room.

'However long is it going to take to make the place habitable?' I asked anxiously. 'M. is only giving us two weeks' grace.'

Peter was confident. 'Don't worry. I'll send in a team of my chaps for a few days to clean the place up ahead of the P.W.D. workmen. Then it shouldn't take longer than a week. Come on: we'd better go.'

'But we haven't looked at the kitchen yet,' I protested.

'I shouldn't bother. It'll have to be sorted out anyway. We'd better dash if we want a couple of sets at the Club before curfew.'

With the trouble continuing all over the country, curfews were in operation in the main centres of population, and although we felt no animosity against us, as expatriates, it was still unnerving to see armed soldiers at every corner and jeeps touring the town.

We were in the middle of an exceptionally hot spell, even though the rains had begun a month earlier, but despite the heat I was so delighted to be well again after the unexpected onslaught and defeat of my old enemy, strongyloides, I played tennis as often and for as long as possible. On the afternoon of our visit to Nassarawa Road, I squeezed in five hard-fought sets before we hurried home without even stopping for a cool drink or to change out of my tennis dress which was sopping wet with perspiration.

Next morning, when I attempted to get up, my legs felt strangely weak and my hands and arms began tingling madly. At the same time the old familiar crawling sensation of five years ago started up the back of my neck and to my horror my thumbs tightened and began to move, involuntarily across my palms.

'O God! No!' I cried.

Peter thrust me into the car and drove at top speed to the hospital where within minutes I was on a drip and being reassured by a smiling Nigerian doctor. 'It's only a salt and mineral deficiency,' he said. 'You'll be fine by tonight and be able to go home tomorrow. Come to my surgery for a check-up the day after.'

Dr Mama ran a private surgery at his home on the far side of the town, but it was not simply for one check-up that I had to be taken there. During the following fortnight there were frequent recurrences, despite a plethora of pills – calcium, salts, vitamins etc., and twice we had to run the gauntlet of the curfew, with me huddled on the floor of the car and Peter keeping as low behind the wheel as humanly possible, fearing to be fired on by trigger-happy Hausa soldiers on duty all round Kaduna. But we were lucky. The excellent Dr Mama arranged tests, prescribed a variety of medicines and supervised my treatment with the utmost care and concern until I recovered, just in time for the move into No. 16 Nassarawa.

Peter had detailed four labourers to do the initial scrubbing-out. With gallons of disinfectant, a carton of carbolic soap and a dozen scrubbing brushes, they spent a full week removing the excrement in the bathrooms and leaving them ready for the P.W.D. team.

Mr Carter promised that painters, plumbers and carpenters would get to work immediately, and the whole place would be put to rights in plenty of time for our move.

The alarm over my illness and the consequent frequent dashes to the surgery, plus his heavy workload of detailed survey reports to finish, made it impossible for Peter to visit the house again before M–Day, so when it arrived and, having deposited the children with friends, we took our loads to Nassarawa, it was exasperating beyond words to find that nothing, beyond some cursory painting over the worst areas, had been started. The inevitable absence of a telephone meant that Peter had to drive straight round to the P.W.D. supervisor's office to demand immediate and urgent action on all fronts, while I sat in the dingy reception room on a suitcase, gloomily surveying the scene.

Three quarters of an hour later, Peter returned, closely followed into the drive by an ancient lorry from which scrambled half a dozen workmen carrying an assortment of tools, brushes, tins of paint, lengths of wire and flex and odd bits of timber.

The rest of that day and the whole of the week were like a Marx brothers' film, though we found it hard to see the funny side, at least until it was all over.

My first concern was that the 'chicken hut' in the main bedroom be restored to its intended function as a wardrobe. 'No savvy this thing; be bad past all,' commented the carpenter shaking his head as he duly removed the mesh, cleaned up the droppings and swept up the last of the feathers. As he replaced the doors which had been left lying on the floor in a corner of the room I lifted the lid of the first case, thankful that at last I could start putting things away. Finding the bag of hangers, I went to the wardrobe to put them up only to find that there was no rail.

I hared downstairs and caught the carpenter as he was leaving the house and explained that the job was not finished. 'Be no wood for rail here, Madam,' he said. 'I go for back and bring wood soon.'

For a further hour I sat on a box and watched the men, who, without guidance from any visible quarter, wandered from room to room laughing and chatting until Peter's patience gave out and he led them to the next most urgent of the hundred and one jobs to do to make the place habitable.

At last the carpenter came through the front door carrying a long pole over his shoulder. As he swung it round to climb the stairs, the electrician working at the foot of the staircase had to duck to avoid being hit. He succeeded, but the end of the pole smashed into the new light switch that had just been wired in, and pieces of fitting clattered to the floor. 'Aiee!' exclaimed the carpenter, realising what he had done, but as he turned back quickly, the pole swung the other way, its rear end catching a workman on the wrist with a sharp crack. Unfortunately, the man was decorating and it was the hand that was holding the paint tin .....

Meanwhile the polisher had arrived to deal with the furniture in the main reception room. 'No, not that sofa,' said Peter seeing the man working on its wooden arms. 'It's broken. Look.' He pointed to the trailing springs. 'It's going to be taken away and another brought. It's the chairs that need attention.'

'No sah. Boss tell me he say – Ali, you polish sofa good. No chairs. Dey go for back.'

'We can't use that sofa!' Peter exploded. 'The damn thing's useless! Mr Carter told me he would replace it! In fact the new one should be here, *now!*'

We watched helplessly as the polisher continued working on the damaged sofa. Ignoring the chairs which, though dirty and smelly, were saveable if the wooden arms had their scratches and stains dealt with and the cushions renewed, he moved to the dining room. 'He's never going to do anything to that table!' I felt quite desperate.

'Dis here be fine table, Madam. I make'um ver' good,' he said confidently, rubbing lightly and ineffectually over the charred, indented surface.

And so it continued. He 'polished' the furniture we had been assured would be replaced, and refused to touch the items that we knew were to remain. I couldn't bear to watch and went back upstairs in the hope of finding the rail fixed in the wardrobe. Greatly relieved when I opened the doors, there it was, and I began hanging up my cotton frocks. Feeling more cheered, I filled the rail and closed the doors while fetching shoes and sandals from one of the boxes to put at the bottom. Returning to the wardrobe, I opened the doors again. All the dresses lay in a heap on the floor and the new rail made a neat diagonal from the left of the pile to the right-hand top corner....

Peter came running upstairs in answer to my shriek. 'Leave it,' he said comfortingly. 'Let's get Mohammedu to make us a cup of tea, then I'll catch hold of that carpenter and drive round to the P.W.D. office.'

We sat forlornly on two of our own camp chairs, surveying the mess all round us, when the steward ran in from the kitchen. 'Be no water, sah. Tap he be gone, sah.'

Peter raised his eyebrows and sighed. 'I'll go and find Mr Carter right now,' he said. 'Obviously we've got to have water, so I'll bring a plumber back with me.'

'Be plumber here, sah,' said one of the painters. 'Be fixing latrine.' He pointed to one of the bathrooms.

'Thank goodness for that,' said Peter, who was on the point of losing his normal calm. He explained the problem to the man.

'I fix 'um pretty dam' quick,' he grinned and disappeared into the kitchen, reappearing without the grin within seconds. 'No tap, sah,' he said. 'I look 'um, I see 'um. I no find 'um sah.'

'I know there's no tap!' Peter was definitely losing his cool. 'I told you!' he said in dangerous whisper that rose rapidly to a repressed shout. 'I told you we couldn't get water *because the tap's gone*! please get one *now!*'

'*Yessah.*' The man's eyes rolled and he glanced at the kitchen door as if making sure that a quick exit was available if needed. 'I unnerstan'. Hurry one time, sah.' And he shot through the door.

'Well he seems to have got the message now,' said Peter and sure enough, within twenty minutes, Mohammedu came in bearing a much-needed tray of tea. 'At last!' we said simultaneously. 'They must have fixed the tap. Have they? That was quick.' I poured the tea.

'Yes, Madam.' Mohammedu's face showed his own relief. An excellent steward who took pride in his work, he was always concerned if he wasn't able to look after us with his normal efficiency.

'Thank you very much. Now you can go off for a couple of hours. You've had a hard day too, and you'll want to get your own quarters fixed up.'

'Thank you, sah.' The steward went off to his own rooms which were in a separate building in the back garden to the side of the long 'wives' walkway'. We settled down to our tea and watched the workmen who, far from finished, were packing up for the day.

'We'll just have to camp here for a bit,' said Peter ruefully. 'Mr Carter's promises obviously mean nothing and it looks as if it will take at least a week to get the place straight.'

'Oh well,' I said resignedly, 'At least the children will think it's fun.'

We had barely sipped our first cup when Mohammedu burst back into the room. 'Sah! Come quick! There be water, plenty water too much, sah!'

Peter jumped up and swiftly followed Mohammedu, who appeared to be extremely distressed, to his quarters.

Within minutes he was back, nearly purple with anger. 'You'll never believe this,' he shouted as he ran out to the car. 'I've got to get that bloody plumber back here *now*! Instead of getting a new tap to put in the kitchen, he went to Mohammedu's room and pinched *his*! The whole place is flooded! All his stuff is soaking wet and the water's gushing out like Niagara! I don't know where the bloody stopcock is, even!'

The tyres squealed as he scorched out of the drive and I offered up a silent prayer for his safety, our sanity... and Mohammedu's patience in adversity.

❦❦❦❦

It was more than a month before No. 16 was decently habitable; a month of continuous battle with the P.W.D. to get usable furniture, to have the hundred-and-one repair jobs finished, to find and get made up eighty yards of curtain fabric. Problems were exacerbated by the maddening delay in the despatch of our loads from Lagos where they sat for six weeks. When they finally turned up, the keys were missing and Peter had to smash the locks. But at least we could unpack properly and partly furnish the barn-like rooms.

Unfortunately our tribulations were not over. One morning a large, shiny limousine drew up outside the front door and as I went out to greet the unexpected visitors, the car – a taxi – disappeared out of the drive and its passengers went scurrying round the side of the house. Following them and wondering what on earth was going on, I saw them running down the path towards Mohammedu's quarters, then scoot across to the long wall of the 'wives' walk-way', sidling along it until they slipped through a door into the former women's compound. We knew that squatters had moved into several neighbouring compounds and were causing endless trouble, so Peter enquired of the Housing Officer if these new arrivals were legitimate tenants. Oh yes, he said, they were junior civil servants who had been allocated the premises. At first we were reassured and expected no bother. It was just amusing that they obviously liked to pretend to the world at large that they were the real occupants of 'the big house', as they swept right up to the grand entrance in taxis or their own large but, shabby jalopies, then slunk round the back hoping no one noticed their true destination.

In fact there was an official and direct path provided for their use off a minor road which skirted the rear gardens of the Ministers' houses, giving access to the former women's quarters. We had no inkling that our 'tenants' were hatching a plan to change this arrangement following the Housing Officer's ban on their use of the main entrance.

But their first direct encroachment on our lives came on another front. We couldn't help noticing that their compound was ablaze with lights all night and all day. Music blared continuously from radios and gramophones, luckily too far away to bother us overmuch, but we began to be concerned when the long linking corridor was also permanently lit up, and loud music and voices could be heard through the interconnecting door.

Then came an electricity bill – the first since the tenants' arrival. It was simply unbelievable. Peter refused to pay and demanded that someone come to the house and explain why the expected charges had quadrupled.

The answer was not long in coming. 'I think we've met this situation before, sir,' said the inspector, stroking his ginger moustache as he walked around the outside of the house, having already carefully checked the few electrical items we used. Back inside the house he asked, 'Have you a key?' He pointed to the door leading to the wives' corridor. Peter opened it and the inspector nodded. 'Look at this,' he said, pointing to a wire dangling between two meters up on the wall a few feet from the door. They've just bypassed the one we installed for them, and hooked up to yours, I'm afraid.' We were shocked. He grinned wryly. 'You are not alone. I've found three identical cases in this road in the past two weeks. Don't worry. We'll sort your bill out – and deal with these blighters.' With a cheery wave he was gone.

❧❧❧❧

'Bloody hell! ... Damn and blast them!' Peter was not easily roused, so I was alarmed when I heard him sounding off in fury yet again, as he stormed back into the house only a few minutes after leaving it. His Kaduna routine was to do an early stint at HQ from 7 a.m., returning to breakfast at 9 for an hour before going back to the office until 2.30 p.m. His workload was so heavy that only a major problem would interfere with it, and he often worked several hours in the evening too.

'They're back!' he shouted, throwing his brief-case onto the table with such force that all the cups and plates jumped.

'Oh God, no!' I put my head in my hands in despair. The latest and most serious aggravation from the tenants in the former womens' quarters was the hiring of unofficial 'contractors' to build a road leading off our drive to their own door, demolishing the garden in the process. Negotiation had proved fruitless and now we had daily battles with the dozen or so labourers who turned up every morning in an ancient truck laden with picks and spades. The gardener and I had spent nearly two months clearing and planting, in the face of frequent invasions by donkeys, goats, cow-Fulani children herding a few of their patiently lumbering beasts, as well as streams of people on their way to and from the nearby market, or sabon gari, who had found it a useful short cut while the house stood empty. With Ali providing most of the muscle-power, we'd established rosebeds, planted clumps of canna lilies fronted by carpets of portulaca, laid a new plumbago hedge, tidied up the various old bougainvilleas and rescued several allamandas from near-extinction.

We had just begun to see the fruits of all our labours when, returning from a morning at the pool followed by a picnic with friends, we were greeted by a scene of devastation, a truck parked on the top of the new central rosebed where a few crushed twigs poked forlornly from under its wheels. A gang of men, all stripped to the waist, heaved at the ground with mattocks or shovels, digging up the newly-planted shrubs and flowers and tossing them aside, while two or three others sat gossipping on a pile of bricks – evidently the remains of a large chunk of the garden wall.

Peter drove at speed to the P.W.D. Superintendent's office. No, he was told, the road had not been sanctioned by anyone. It was quite illegal. The Police would have to deal with it. 'Will you report it, then?' he asked.

'No. Much better if you sort it out. You're on the spot.'

Report it he did, immediately, and came back with the encouraging news that the police would be round within the hour. After delivering a stern warning to the foreman, Peter collected his briefcase and prepared to go to the office.

'That should take care of that,' he said, giving me a comforting hug. 'We'll ask Ali to increase his hours for a bit and I'm sure you and he will have a lovely garden again in no time.'

Too upset to take another look at the ruination outside, I put the children down for a nap and waited for the constables, who, as promised, arrived within the hour. Hearing their car roar into the drive, tyres squealing, I hurried out to greet them and take them to the scene, but as they stepped out of their vehicle, there came a sudden stuttering clank from the old lorry behind the house, shouts and thwacks as implements were thrown into the back, the workmen leapt in with them and it rattled out of the garden at speed through the gap where the wall had been knocked down.

'Good. No more trouble I think,' said one of the policemen, smiling broadly. Turning on their heels, they went straight back to their vehicle and scorched out of the drive. Not wholly reassured, I went back into the house, but there was no sign of the work gang during the remainder of the afternoon, so I began to hope that the threat of police intervention was going to do the trick.

This fond hope was short-lived. At eight next morning the truck rolled up and the business of devastation recommenced as if nothing had occurred to interrupt it. My protests, translated by Mohammedu, were completely ignored: the men just grinned at each other. 'Right!' said Peter grimly as soon as he came in for breakfast and saw what was happening. 'I'm going to the station now and will bring the police back with me!'

As soon as he had gone, Mohammedu came to me. 'I think these bad men go for back when police come, Madam. One man he watch from side of house.'

The steward was quite right. The moment Peter reappeared, bringing the same two policemen with him, the labourers tossed their tools into the already moving truck, chased like mad to catch it up and threw themselves in. Some only managed to cling on with their fingertips but all were laughing at our discomfiture as they hurtled off at full throttle.

Peter was beside himself. The policemen shrugged and returned to the car, waiting silently to be taken back to the station. No suggestions were made or advice offered.

Over the next three days this pantomime was repeated many times. It rapidly became an embarrassment to ask for police assistance, as on each occasion the gang returned within minutes of the constables' departure. We were at our wits' end, and I was extremely worried that Peter, besides being in a state of continuous anger, was also sacrificing precious time from his project, which undoubtedly meant even more pressure of work over the coming weeks.

Something drastic was needed.

On the morning of the fourth day there was no sign of them by the time Peter was ready to return to the office after breakfast, and we began to hope that someone in authority had finally prevailed on them to stop.

He went off more cheerfully than he'd been for days but his premature return and furious outburst were the result of meeting the lorry half way along Nassarawa Road, and he'd pulled up to watch where it went.

'Look,' I said, trying to calm him down, upset as I was myself, 'I have a plan. You go and fetch the police and I'll prevent the lorry leaving the garden.'

He looked at me doubtfully. 'I can't imagine how you could stop these blighters.'

'I can and I will,' I said. 'And it's our only hope of putting an end to this ridiculous situation.'

'O.K. you can try, but for heaven's sake don't do anything rash.'

As expected, a few minutes after the disappearance of Peter's car in the direction of the police station, the labourers began hastily piling their tools into the back of the lorry and prepared for their usual getaway.

'Quick, Mohammedu!' I called. 'Get the deckchair now-now, please!'

Already primed to the stratagem, our faithful steward carried a sturdy garden chair out onto the roughly flattened track where the flower beds had been annihilated and placed it carefully barely five feet in front of the ramshackle vehicle, too close for it to manoeuvre round.

'*What you do*?" cried the driver angrily, leaping down from the cab.

'Madam wish to sit in garden,' said Mohammedu, and he stood behind the chair with his hands on the back as if he was a waiter assisting a diner in a restaurant, as I sat down with my book on my lap. As I opened it, I whispered to him to leave me, ostensibly ignoring the popping eyes and the excited jabbering from the men in the back.

He moved away, but evidently rather anxious, stayed well within earshot.

The driver approached and bent over me. 'Madam, dis be big mistake! We go for back!'

I looked up. There were little globules of sweat running down the sides of his face, and the skin was taut across his flat nose. He was plainly panicky. I smiled at him. 'This is a very interesting book. I'm going to sit here *all morning* and read it.'

He turned away in exasperation and jumped into the cab. With an ear-splitting noise, like the rattle of a machine-gun salvo, the engine burst into life.

With an outward show of calm indifference that was sorely lacking inside me, I turned over a page of my book.

The reverberations continued for a minute or so, then stopped. The driver tried a different tack.

'Madam be thirsty, yes? Like to get nice cold drink from house?'

'No thank you very much,' I replied, not looking up.

The engine was instantly switched on again; this time the racket was accompanied by the crashing of gears.

I held my breath. Slowly the lorry inched towards me.

He won't run me down, I told myself firmly. He wouldn't be so insane. It's one thing to defy the law by trespassing and damaging Government property, but causing deliberate injury – or worse – to the wife of a senior Government officer .....

All the same, it took a great effort of will to take my eyes from the book, which somehow seemed to be an insurance of my safety, and look up at the driver with what I hoped was an air of quizzical nonchalance. From where I sat he was only just visible, peering down over the upper rim of the steering wheel, as the rusty radiator was now only six inches from my legs.

For several seconds we each attempted to outface each other. Then the engine spluttered and stopped – deliberately or seized I couldn't tell.

Wearily he climbed down from the cab again. 'Be too hot here, Madam. Too much hot. You sit in shade, yes?' He was beginning to lack conviction and I felt encouraged.

'A good idea,' I said cheerfully, and called the steward. 'Mohammedu, could you bring the garden umbrella, please?'

'Yes Madam,' he called back laughing, and within moments he was standing beside the chair holding the umbrella over my head and trying to keep his face straight.

Just as it crossed my mind that I couldn't keep Mohammedu standing out in the sun, and was wondering how long I could maintain this absurdity without it developing into something really serious, we heard the blare of approaching police car sirens and the gang was galvanised into action. Some had squatted on their hunkers beside the lorry, others had hung over the sides, watching bemusedly the farce played out by the crazy European Madam and their infuriated boss-man.

Now they scarpered, haring off in all directions, abandoning the lorry, their implements and each other. By the time the four policemen had run round from the front of the house and sent another two to block the 'emergency exit' through the hole in the garden wall, the birds had flown. For a short distance they pursued some of the fleeing figures, but soon gave up and came back to congratulate themselves on having 'captured' the lorry and all the equipment.

We were confidently assured that 'these bad men' would be rounded up and brought to trial. No mention was made of the tenants who had instigated the whole business – and who must have been financing it.

Like so many 'fiddles' in Nigeria, it seemed that palms had been greased and, as usual, the real perpetrators would escape justice.

Hope that our privacy would be restored and that life in Minister's Row might now be without further aggravation was short-lived. While the workmen did not reappear, the half-made road and the large gap in the garden wall offered an open invitation to all and sundry. It was an ideal cut-through to the nearby market, avoiding a tediously roundabout route.

Nicola and Joanna were fascinated by the sight of indignant fowls tied in bunches by their feet and squawking their annoyance at having their beaks trail in the dust, goats pulled on strings by children no older than themselves, packs of skinny yellow dogs tied together and yelping when the man dragging them behind him tugged viciously at the cords around their necks.

Our two worried about the dogs. 'Where are they going, Mummy?' asked Nicola.

'They must be hunting dogs,' I answered doubtfully. 'Probably going to be sold and taken out to bush somewhere.' (I learnt later that my misgivings were justified and they were being taken to market for quite another purpose.)

There were also the inevitable donkeys with enormous loads on their backs or baskets strapped to their sides, urged on with cruel beatings and shouts; other big loads were carried by quite small children who seemed unconcerned by the bulky packages on their heads.

The daily spectacle would have been entertaining had *we* not been the objects of curiosity, too: it was disconcerting to see noses pressed to the sitting room windows and round-eyed gaze taking in our domestic scene. The normally placid Mohammedu was frequently made irate having to chase away inquisitive picans from the kitchen door and, with his own quarters now separated from the main house by the 'road', he was naturally uneasy about the security of his belongings, especially as the village on the other side of Nassarawa Road was notorious for its 'teef-men'.

We decided enough was enough.

Sympathy from friends and colleagues included offers of houses we could have while their usual occupants were on leave.

We gratefully accepted that of a senior officer in the Veterinary Department and made the quickest and easiest of our Nigerian shifts (by this time numbering about twenty-five). We found a comfortable house and a large garden full of flowering trees and shrubs. The accommodation at first seemed somewhat cramped after the expanse of No. 16, but it was more than adequate and a joy to escape from a 'goldfish bowl' existence and daily tensions.

Both the girls were able to join the handful of other expat. children at the multi-racial Capital School, and I was asked to teach there.

It was time for annual tests for my 7–9 year-olds, and they provided the usual quota of howlers; the one I liked best was the answer to the question – 'How does a Fulani herdsman spend his time?' .... 'With women.'

A lesson we all looked forward to was the weekly session at the Hamdallah Hotel pool, but to reach it we had to walk through the grounds where we ran the gauntlet of the tiresome resident ostrich. One little boy, the offspring of an 80-year-old father and a mother barely in her teens, had an extraordinarily-shaped head, just like a large coconut, which the wretched bird always made a beeline for. Poor Abu was naturally terrified when the huge bird ran up and began pecking viciously at his crown, while I, just as frightened, tried to shoo it away and get my nervous 'crocodile' safely through the gate to the poolside.

Another, bigger scare came towards the end of' the first lesson.

Before leaving the classroom and again at the pool, I stressed the vital importance of obeying instructions exactly, and *never* going into the water without permission. Most of the class were from traditional, though wealthy, Nigerian homes and had never been to a swimming pool before.

The lesson progressed happily. The half-dozen European children were confident, independent swimmers, so until the final five minutes I devoted my attention to the timorously excited African majority group, when I told them it was time to get out and go and dress. I watched them all file into the changing rooms, then turned to the swimmers.

'You can all have a few minutes on the diving boards or go down the chute,' I said, knowing they were all used to the deep end and feeling they deserved a little treat, having been confined to the shallow end while I concentrated on the non-swimmers.

I supervised, coached and admired all the tricks they usually tried when they came with their families and friends, but time was up so I agreed to one more turn each down the chute and sent them, one by one, in to change.

The last child was disappearing through the door and I was about to follow and chivvy everyone up when, out of the corner of my eye, I caught sight of a small *black* figure whizzing down the chute into 14 feet of water. Dashing back to the poolside, I could see no sign of Ahmedu (I had guessed who it probably was), and for a few terrifying seconds I feared he must be lying on the bottom, but then I made out a dark, spreadeagled shape, face down, unmoving, about a foot below the surface. As it began gradually to sink again, the paralysing shock which had momentarily rooted me to the spot, lifted, and I hurled myself into the water and grabbed him before he was lost to sight again.

I had not had to use my life-saving skills in earnest before, but he was light and I quickly got him to the bar and heaved him out on to the side. Luckily he was conscious and he lay for a couple of minutes coughing and spluttering. As soon as he had recovered sufficiently, I sent him to the changing room with a furious telling-off – the result of my own fright. He was unfazed. I'm afraid he was another of those sad innocents whom Nature had never imagined would be conceived. When my equilibrium was restored I felt very guilty about my outburst, but it was never held against me: his habitual vacant smile remained intact.

❧❧❧❧

Smiles were back on the faces of the Hausa people, now that their traditional enemies had been eliminated from their region either by murder or persecution.

For the Ibos, however, the nightmare of the widespread massacres in the North and the sad flight of survivors back to their homeland in the East was soon to be succeeded by renewed and prolonged suffering.

As expatriates, we were largely insulated from the seething turmoil of Nigerian politics, now rapidly approaching boiling point. The local television station's output was mostly parochial, tending to the trivial. While Col. Ojukwu threatened secession, seized Federal services and banished all Northerners from the East, our own small daughters were happily engaged in extra dancing classes in preparation for a televised performance.

In November, the East began buying arms from whoever would supply them, and Ojukwu reacted to the announcement by the Commander-in Chief, Col. Gowon, that the country was to be subdivided into many small states, three of them in the East, by refusing to cooperate, and ordering all Federal troops to leave the Eastern and Western Regions.

December in Kaduna was spent frantically rehearsing for a Christmas Concert by the local Music Society, also to be shown on T.V. It was a mixture of traditional carols, Peter Warlock and 'I'm Dreaming of a White Christmas', followed in January by auditions for an ambitious production of *The Gondoliers*; at the same time, in Aburi, near Accra, a meeting of Nigeria's military leaders, initiated by the Head of the Military Government in Ghana, appeared to have produced an agreement acceptable to both Col. Gowon and the Ibo leader, but it was soon repudiated by the government in Lagos.

Ojukwu accused Gowon of betrayal. He demanded direct payment of Federal taxes and oil revenues, and in May, with a considerable military force, great resources of oil and the support of many smaller tribes, sealed the borders and declared secession of the 'Republic of Biafra'.

Gowon promptly announced that his plan of splitting the country into twelve states would be enacted in a year's time. This had the effect of reducing the support Ojukwu had received from the minorities as this offered them the sovereignty they'd long agitated for. However, a Federal effort to take the region in a speedy 'police operation' failed; instead it marked the beginning of a terrible war of attrition in which at least a million and a half Ibo civilians died, many massacred, tens or hundreds of thousands from starvation. By August 1968 the *daily* mortality rate was six thousand, and only six million Ibos were left in a homeland that had been ruthlessly constricted to an area of only sixty miles by forty – one-tenth of its original size.

Yet still the savagery continued. Whether the starvation of the civilian population was the fault of heartless senior figures in Lagos, or the result of Biafran distrust of Nigerian offers to let aid through *provided* Federal forces supervised it, was hotly disputed at the time, and probably still is.

Somehow the remnants of the Ibo people held out for another year and a half, but in January 1970 their heroic resistance ended. Ojukwu fled. Biafra, 'The Land of the Rising Sun' was no more.

By that time my own engagement with Africa had become a distant memory. After the applause for the children's dancing demonstration had died down and the Kaduna choir's struggle with Warlock and 'White Christmas' had been duly criticised – favourably on the whole – our minds turned anxiously towards those auditions, but any aspirations I may have held in that direction were smartly nipped in the bud by the onset of – now familiar – 24-hour-a-day sickness. Number three was on the way, dropping me straight into the black hole of misery in which I had spent most of the two previous pregnancies. Where on earth was this wonderful 'bloom of glowing health and happiness' that mums-to-be were supposed to enjoy?

By March I'd lost more than two stone, and Peter was advised that I ought to be packed off to the U.K. Flights were booked and in a pathetic daze I filled suitcases for the girls while their father wired my parents to have warm clothes ready for their arrival.

Leaving Kaduna at sundown on March 12th we drove the 160-odd miles to Kano airport, arriving at 11.30 p.m., two hours before take-off. Peter left us sitting on our cases at the entrance while he went to find the check-in desk and to ask for a pass so that he could accompany us to the departure lounge.

After about fifteen minutes he returned, puzzled and empty-handed, The check-in point was unmanned, there was no one at passport Control, nor Customs, neither at the Security Zone where presumably one obtained a pass. In fact he'd seen no one at all, except for one or two other bewildered passengers searching for someone to sign them in, weigh their luggage, hand over boarding passes and direct them accordingly.

With legs like cotton-wool and feeling intensely miserable in spite of the prospect of at last going home, I leaned on Peter as he struggled with luggage, children and an increasing anxiety about the absence of officials in any capacity. Following overhead signs, we trailed along bare, echoing corridors, past empty desks, under uplifted barriers beside deserted cubicles. An eerie silence hung over the place.

Finally we came to double doors marked Departure Lounge, and underneath, 'No Admittance Without Pass'. Peter shrugged. 'There's no one to get a pass from, I'll have to take you in. There's no one else here.'

We trudged into the empty room and sat down wearily. It was past midnight and still more than an hour to wait. The minutes dragged by. Nicola and Joanna curled up together on a sofa and slept in fits and starts, while I closed my eyes and dreamed of being well, safe and confident again, no longer the chicken-hearted pessimist I had become. Within an hour, I and my precious children would be free of this unpredictable, intimidating land. It would only be a few months before Peter could join us and we'd be a normal family with an exciting future to look forward to on our small Norfolk farm. Peter frequently said he was finished with Africa, even after the recent agreeable surprise of seeing himself headlined, with Phil, in Northern newspapers, above glowing accounts of their mammoth work for Nigeria. Now I believed him.

❧❧❧❧

Lucky me! The curtain had finally come down on the scenario of continual crisis since our marriage in '58...

My drowsy fancies were interrupted by the sound of imperiously snapping fingers above me.

With head still slumped forward, I opened my eyes to see a pair of highly-polished toecaps confronting my own well-worn sandals; the razor-sharp creases of military-style trousers bent slightly as the hems rose and fell with the lifting and heavy falling of heels in impatient rhythm.

As the usual waves of nausea washed over me, it was some moments before I could look up, to see Peter already on his feet, teeth clenched in indignation, as the officer – if that was what he was, with his gold-braided service dress cap, immaculate uniform, gleaming buttons and gold epaulettes wagged an accusing finger, demanding to see our passes.

Vainly Peter tried to explain that no one was available to issue passes, that he could not abandon a sick wife and small children without leaving them in responsible hands, that no personnel had been at their posts for check-in or to see to our luggage. This squat, sneering little man with bulging eyes above shiny fat cheeks twirled his swagger-stick and pointed it menacingly at each of us.

'You know, I can arrest you *now*!' He spoke gloatingly, relishing his position of power. 'You'll get two years in prison at least for this.'

With the greatest difficulty Peter held his tongue while I tried, unsuccessfully, to hide my panicky tears, praying that the children wouldn't wake. But this bully was determined that they should.

He began ranting at the top of his voice.

'You Europeans think you can do anything! You walk all over us, treat us like dirt! But who's got the *brains*? Who got the aeroplane first? Yet when we take charge of our own country, you colonials still expect us to lick your boots!'

The children woke, terrified to witness this arrogant belligerent man threatening their father, and ran to me, sobbing.

This sign of evident weakness spurred him to further bombastic sabre-rattling, and while I cuddled the whimpering little ones and Peter struggled to maintain his self-control, the diatribe – the threats continually increasing in severity and now including an 'instant fine' of £4000 – reached a shrill peak of vitriol.

Suddenly it stopped. An air hostess had slipped into the room and was coming smilingly towards us.

Our tormentor drew himself up to his full 5ft. 2in. height, clicked his heels, bowed, then with an oily smirk, wished us goodnight.

'Enjoy your flight, madam,' he said to me. And left.

POSTSCRIPT

During the fraught period spent in the Eastern Transvaal, we were directed by friends to a 'Wise Woman' who would 'throw the bones' for us.

Unfortunately I recorded no details of this extraordinary encounter in my diary, neither did I include it in my letters to my parents, probably because her predictions at the time appeared to be quite implausible, and bore no relation to our plans.

Dressed in traditional robes, colourfully beaded and with a quiet air of calm, I remember that she took a handful of small objects from a leather pouch at her waist and cast them across the earth-trodden floor of her hut.

We could see no significance in the odd assortment, which included birds' claws, shells, pebbles as well as little bones, as I recall, but after studying the random pattern for a few minutes, she began to describe with uncanny accuracy our families, our lives and our current situation.

Our amazement, however, turned to scepticism when, after some hesitation, she spoke of our future. At that time we were confident of remaining in Africa: Swaziland beckoned, and the prophecy of a life-changing journey of thousands of miles to make our home in a distant land within two years, seemed ridiculously off-target. Consequently we were unperturbed by the further prediction that our lives would be blighted by ill-health and early death though she did not specify the sufferer.

Afterwards we looked laughingly at the life lines on our palms and could see nothing untoward; my long-term dysentery seemed better and Peter was blessed with an exceptionally tough physique. So we thought...

The Swaziland venture ended within eighteen months, when Peter returned to the U.K. and bought Orchard Farm. Then, after his two years' work on the World Bank project he attempted to farm our few acres, but in his late forties developed Parkinson's Disease. During the next twelve years, with our elder daughter also becoming chronically ill, his condition deteriorated and became critical after he was involved in a serious road accident. Months of pain and gradual paralysis followed, ending with his death in 1990.